The Cold Fire

The Cold Fire

Alienation and the Myth of Culture
by Stanley D. Rosenberg and
Bernard J. Bergen

Published for Dartmouth College

by the University Press of New England

Hanover, New Hampshire 1976

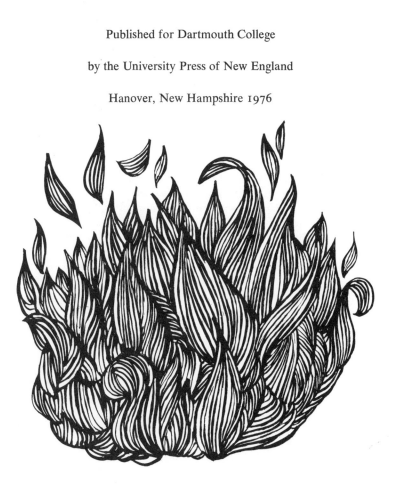

Permissions have been granted for reprinting extracts
from the following works:
Big Sky Music, "When I Paint My Masterpiece,"
© 1971, 1972, by Big Sky Music.
Delacorte Press/Seymour Lawrence, *The Sirens of Titan*,
by Kurt Vonnegut, Jr., © 1959 by Kurt Vonnegut, Jr.
Harper and Row, *The Raw and the Cooked: Introduction to a
Science of Mythology*, Volume I, by Claude Levi-Strauss,
© 1964 by Harper and Row.
International Universities Press, *The Eternal Ones of the Dream*,
by Geza Roheim, © 1945 by International Universities Press.
International Universities Press, *Psychoanalysis and Anthropology*,
by Geza Roheim, © 1950 by International Universities Press.
Little, Brown and Co., *The Middle Americans*, by Robert Coles,
© 1971 by Robert Coles.
Macmillan Publishing Co., Inc., *Symbolic Wounds*,
by Bruno Bettelheim, © 1954 by The Free Press.
Random House, Inc., *Invisible Man*, by Ralph Ellison,
© 1952 by Random House.
Viking Press, Inc., (Viking Penguin, Inc.), *Herzog*,
by Saul Bellow, © 1961, 1963, 1964 by Saul Bellow.

For Harriet and Vera

Preface

This book evolved from our interests in two spheres. The first was the work of several psychoanalytically grounded social theorists: Norman O. Brown (*Love's Body, Life against Death*), Herbert Marcuse (*Eros and Civilization*), and Philip Rieff (*The Triumph of the Therapeutic*). All three writers are concerned with the relation of culture, society, and the unconscious. All three grapple with the question why modern cultures produce so much self-estrangement. Bernard Bergen had spent a number of years studying their theses and comparing them, one with another and with the works of Freud. He shared some of his thinking on these issues with a graduate seminar at Yale University in 1966. As a member of that seminar, Stanley Rosenberg found that he shared with Bergen the belief that these writers were pointing to the most profound questions yet posed about man's relation to culture.

The first product of our mutual interest was a paper published in *Psychiatry* in 1971.* Meanwhile, we had become increasingly interested in the social upheavals of the late 1960's and early 70's. The issues raised by Brown, Marcuse, and Rieff were being played out and debated all around us. We became as much interested in the phenomenon of contemporary alienation itself as with the theorists who were attempting to place it within a causal framework. This second line of study led to

---

*Bernard J. Bergen and Stanley D. Rosenberg, "The New Neo-Freudians: Psychoanalytic Dimensions of Social Change," *Psychiatry*, 34:1 (1971).

a greater appreciation of phenomenology and existentialism (especially the works of Laing, Sartre, Kierkegaard, and Heidegger) as an approach that could help us to appreciate better the experience of alienation. More to the point, we became avid readers of statements of alienation themselves. The experience of alienation, we came to feel, was not reducible to any theoretical formulation. The experience has an intrinsic meaning that can best be appreciated on its own terms.

The book that follows, proceeding on that assumption, tries to present sufficient source material for the reader to enter into the experience. There is great diversity in the material we present; novels, song lyrics, biographies, case histories, and myths. The diversity is not random—the material has been selected to emphasize the ubiquity of alienation and despair, and to show the enormous diversity of its expression. In this sense the book is an adumbration of the experience of alienation, self-consciously circling back on itself in order to deepen and specify general lines of analysis begun earlier. We knew of no other way to convey the experience in its multiple guises and in the complexity of its meaning for the despairing self.

We would like to acknowledge the support received by both authors from the Department of Psychiatry, Dartmouth Medical School. Dr. Peter Whybrow was consistently generous in giving us time and encouragement to engage in the writing. A number of colleagues discussed many of the ideas and commented on earlier drafts and chapters. We would like to acknowledge the help that Claudewell Thomas, Michael Farrell, Joan Smith, Jean Schimek, Harry Scarr, Sidney Blatt, Brooks Brenneis, and Irving Janis gave us with their suggestions and criticisms. Virtually every page of the book has been talked out with and commented on by Harriet Rosenberg and Vera Bergen, and their contribution to the final product is substantial.

Hanover, N.H. S.D.R.
May 1976 B.J.B.

Contents

This is the hot incitement,
or the cold fire in despair,
the gnawing canker whose movement
is constantly inward, deeper, and deeper,
in impotent self consumption.

Soren Kierkegaard,
The Sickness unto Death

Introduction

Our aim is to examine the experience of alienation. The term as we use it refers to an interrelated set of perceptions and feelings whereby a person realizes that he is estranged from himself.[1] In the alienated experience one comes to feel like an object under the control of alien forces. These forces can be as general as values or institutions and as specific as the demands of a parent. By capitulating, the self feels transformed into an object. Instead of feeling free, alive, and the agent of one's own choices, he may feel an oppressive deadness.

Alienation always involves two relational components: the relation of the self to itself and the self to the "other." This other (institution or person) may make demands on the self, but it is only when the self becomes enslaved by these demands that it feels alienated from itself. A person may choose to do that which the other requests while experiencing the choice as his own. He feels free, that is, to accept or reject the demand and live with the consequences of his action. One can thus reject a social demand and not feel alienated. He may feel at odds with or estranged from others, but that alone does not constitute alienation. It is when the self begins to define itself through the image that the other has of it that it moves into the position of alienation. He begins to lose the sense of his own agency. Heidegger and Sartre use such terms as "inauthenticity" and "bad faith" in describing this mode of being, which involves a special kind of self-deception.

The person, according to this view, always retains the option of knowing his own possibilities. The very act of surrendering these possibilities is a negation of what the self "knows" to be true—that he is a person and not purely an object. The alienated position consequently involves a sense of despair over the self, which has been surrendered to the other. The self despairs over its weakness in this surrender, and over its inability to break out of bad faith.

We can observe that persons feel this sort of despair over their own existence without perceiving themselves as alienated.[2] They may believe that their despair has other sources. In the modality of bad faith, the self may bemoan the fact that the other does not adequately see one's "objective" attributes: his strength or his righteousness. The despairing self may act on these assumptions, trying to alter its objective relationships until it finds a pattern that erases its inner disquietude. In the impossibility of this pursuit, the self often begins to experience its alienation. It comes to see that its pursuit of the right persona (social, objective self) can be of no benefit in eradicating despair. In these moments the actions that have constituted much of one's being in the world come to look absurd. This sense of absurdity also reveals to the self the madness of a culture which dictates that the self play out such bad faith. And once alienated, the self can see culture only as a continual, pointless violence. The self longs for a new mode of being in the world. One wishes not to be in the mode of object, but rather to become his own human self. If one cannot make this attempt, despair persists. It may even become more profound in its self-recognition. Yet the self may treasure its new awareness, even if it is painful. The act of awareness may come to represent something very positive. If awareness is not in itself freedom from the alienated condition, it can be appreciated at least as a window looking out of the self-enclosed prison that alienation represents.

In the 1960's, as alienation became an increasingly prominent theme in mass culture, it was precisely this liberating potential of the experience which was emphasized. In film, theater, music, and fiction we saw protagonists struggling to free themselves from alienation.[3] Our heroes no longer fought the "hun," the bad guys, or even the frontier. Yossarian and Hawkeye Pierce fought instead against being caught up in the madness and brutality of collective institutions. Their heroism lies in their refusal to define themselves as objects within a larger cultural framework. They insisted on their own humanity, on their right and ability to say no to the demands and definitions of others. Alienation was, in fact, presented as the only stance a sane man could assume in a system that made no sense.

The audience for these statements of protest and despair became increasingly large and more avid. Alienation became a collective obsession, one of the central themes of mass culture. Student uprisings, the Black Panthers, Weathermen, ghetto riots, protests at the Democratic National Convention in Chicago—all filled newspapers and television screens. All were seen as interrelated manifestations of a mood and a movement that was demanding an end to all systems of domination, systems in which human beings objectified themselves and one another. The assumptions—political, economic, cultural, and psychological—by which we ordered our lives were being questioned and denounced. Self-fulfillment, the alienated declared, was to be found outside the demands of the collectivity. At the same time, as the established order was quick to point out, nothing concrete or substantive was put forward to replace what was being aggressively refused. In terms of traditional revolutionary postures, the radicals of the 1960's appeared disorganized, impulsive, and even, in a bizarre way, frightening. They did not adhere to the traditional format of revolutionary messages—that is, they did not call people to mass actions that would alter culture or social structure in a particular direction. They proclaimed, rather, that the single individual, through confronting his own bad faith, could dissolve culture's authority over him. This negation of culture, as opposed to the

3

more traditional exhortations to modify it, was put forth with great urgency. It was expressed as the feeling that our humanity (and perhaps our survival) depended on our lives changing and changing quickly.

One component of these feelings was a sense of hope or excitement. Recognizing their own despair and perceiving the madness and futility of the institutions they had inherited and created, the vocally disaffected felt that alienation could be transcended. There was a belief (wishful and often unarticulated) that immanent social change was about to end each man's separation from himself, his true humanity. In its most hackneyed form we were entering the "age of Aquarius." The communes were one highly visible manifestation of that belief, the Weathermen, another. Although very different in style, both sought to evolve apart from the institutional forms that alienated men from their own lives and from one another. Both movements expected immediate and tangible results.

As we move deeper into the 1970's, many of the manifestations of alienation which surfaced in the previous decade seem naive, sophomoric, even embarrassing. The excesses of the rebels-turned-culture-heroes are puzzling and anachronistic. It becomes difficult to project one's self back even five or eight years to experience the feelings of excitement, awakening, and hope generated by the would-be revolt against the prevailing culture and its institutional forms. The young, we are repeatedly told, are returning to the apathy characteristic of earlier generations.

The upheavals of the decade just ended were not, however, totally ephemeral. The sense of alienation did not spontaneously generate a new program for existence, nor did it provoke a revolution. Although this lack of immediate "results" led many to retreat, the retreat has not been total. Although few at present are openly espousing revolt, many of the radical perceptions and feelings that surfaced in the 1960's still haunt our consciousness. Our images of ourselves and the world have been altered. Alienation has become a more essential and active part of the collective experience. Kurt Vonnegut's *Break-fast of Champions*, less inventive and more venomous and self-derogatory than his earlier books, climbed immediately to the top of the best seller list. The black humor of Heller's *Catch 22* has become the bleak and remorseless dissection of suffering in Heller's *Something Happened*, another 1975 best seller.

The alienation of the early 70's seems to focus on the point-lessness and emptiness of existence while capturing very little of the humor, freedom, and feelings of awakening that ac-companied these perceptions in the earlier decade. The alien-ation of the 60's envisioned the end of belief in culture as the opening up of endless possibility. If it now seems impossible to return to our earlier faith in cultural institutions, this leaves many feeling in limbo rather than free to define themselves. Kierkegaard spoke of two kinds of conscious despair: of de-fiance, in which the individual cannot be the self he wills him-self to be, and of weakness, in which he does not feel himself to be a self (6:182–207).* It is as if the change from the 60's to the 70's constituted a shift from the consciousness of one despair to the other. Mass culture continues to be dominated by images of suffering and madness, but these occur in a con-text where there is no way out. At the end of Heller's *Catch 22* his protagonist, Yossarian, takes a desperate gamble and flees to Sweden in a lifeboat. In the alienated consciousness of the 1970's this act would appear naive. Why should he expect Sweden to be any better? Yossarian's choices, if we can ex-trapolate, are shrinking. He can either acquiesce and act like a good bomber pilot, or choose to end his existence.

One element in this shift is the demise of the belief that social change can serve as the vehicle for ending alienation. Each man has been thrown back upon himself, to live with his own despair or to seek escape from it. Those who tried

---

*Citations in parentheses refer to the sections of numbered refer-ences at the end of each chapter.

to withdraw from, or transform, the social structure have, at least in the popular imagination, returned to it. The ticket back (or the price of staying in) has been acquiescence—willingness to play by the very rules the alienated had called intolerable. Such compromise leads to a need to deny one's sense of despair.

Thus the expressions of despair become more muted and less linked to demands for change, but are probably no less pervasive and no less profound. Perceptions of the absurdity of belief, the unworkability of our collective institutions, of being lost because we lack any visions of positive change, have become so much a part of common parlance that they often go unnoticed. Alienation—the sense that one must find a way of standing separate from culture and its definitions of the self—has paradoxically become a defining quality of contemporary existence. The alienated haunt us by emphasizing the facts that many of us engage in modes of living that are sometimes experienced as unreal, fraudulent, or sleazy. Indeed, we are fascinated by the voices of alienation—confusing as they may sometimes be—in the same way that we are drawn to Kierkegaard and Nietzsche, and for that matter to all the existential writers. In Barrett's terms they explicate for us the "unique experience of the single one, the individual, who chooses to place himself on trial before the gravest question of his civilization" (1:13). The question is that of the value and significance the individual gives to the authority of culture. Novak has invoked the term "mythos" in referring to the social and historical symbol systems that presumably give individuals a "sense of reality"; the mythos, if the self will give himself over to it, provides "criteria for what counts as relevant or evidential in seeing and relating to the world" (7:35). By openly questioning the value of entering the mythos, the alienated put the viability of culture itself on trial. They declare that the struggle with despair is central to our understanding of ourselves.

This declaration challenges our usual definitions of despair.

We have generally defined it as a subject for academic discourse or as a symptom of warped family structure, poverty, or chaotic social change.[4] Seen as a symptom, despair must be treated or avoided rather than listened to. Contemporary alienation declares itself as a view of social reality which deserves to be heard. It demands that we engage it in a dialogue over the assumptions which structure men's lives. This book represents one effort to open that dialogue. In opening a dialogue with alienation, we move closer to traditions in which men have sought to listen to, interpret, and describe experience rather than explain, judge, or ignore it.

Our attempt to comprehend the experience of alienation is based on both psychoanalysis and phenomenological existentialism. Within these frameworks we find a common emphasis on listening to experience and a common ground from which to interpret what one hears. That is, interpretation takes place in the therapeutic model. The interpreter does not wish to tell the subject what he "really means." Rather, he strives to crystallize what the subject is saying to and about himself, and reflect it back so that the speaker feels that his experience has been clarified, not taken over or changed. This represents a way of listening to and encapsulating the experience that the self describes without reference to ultimate causes or ontological schemas.

As we conceive our task, it is not pessimistic. To listen to despair is to enter it and, in a sense, to be despairing—but that is not identical to being pessimistic. We do not know what constitutes human nature, nor can the interpretation of our data define it. We argue that people living in structured groups have always felt alienated from the rules and beliefs by which they have attempted to govern their lives. We do, however, share with many others the tentative belief that people are capable of constructing different realities—realities in which they feel more free and more alive. Such an attempt at self-liberation, at transcending alienation, has yet to succeed on a mass level. The feelings of being sane, real, one's self have

7

been momentary and privatistic. Such moments occur in people's lives, but they represent a resistance to culture. They are not made possible by what culture provides the self.

Le Peters, the protagonist of Bruce Jay Friedman's *The Dick*, is jolted into confronting the intolerable quality of his existence as a public relations man for homicide bureaus. His role as victim and shill becomes so increasingly absurd to him that he must abandon the role and his wife and escape with his daughter. She is the only person with whom he has a truly affective relationship, based on a mutual recognition of humanity and inner needs. The two take the child's goldfish and embark on their trip. She questions if they are "allowed to." Le Peters replies, "I'll check on it later," and reassures her: "They'll love it." The child's response seems measured: "Hey, maybe you're right" (3:279–80).

We do not yet know whether these fleeting moments or acts of transcendence are indicators of what individuals can achieve. They may be illusory, they may represent no more than themselves: brief instances of feeling whole which are embedded in lifetimes where one feels fragmented and despairing. In order to know if these moments represent a different level of being, one may have to gamble for terrifying stakes, to give up the belief that people know the shape of reality, that they know what they want and need. At this moment in history, as we shall discuss, we have great difficulty in sustaining our most fundamental, cherished beliefs. A crucial issue confronts all people in our culture, although they may phrase it in different ways: the issue of whether they can, like Le Peters, dare to start anew; to construct their own lives without either the constraints or aids that define the self through culture. Alienation can neither define nor assure us of this possibility. Alienation is an experience which, if we allow ourselves to listen to it, reveals to us the impoverishing and self-destructive relations we have chosen to construct with ourselves and with others. It is only by becoming conscious of these relations, which we despairingly live out as the reality of our lives in culture, that we can even begin to think of a possibility beyond despair. This possibility may or may not be real. Only by exploring it, both in our thought and in the ways we choose to live our lives, will we know.

The book is organized into two parts: The Self's Struggle to be Itself, and The Struggle to Flee the Self. Each part focuses on an aspect of what alienation tells us about how we construct our own lives and our relations with other men. Part I emphasizes continuous yearning to be free of the bad faith men live out as their life in culture. Part II underlines the fears and modes of self-deception, both individual and cultural, which keep the self enmeshed in the unreality of its despair. The epilogue speaks to the possibility of breaking out of this web.

In Chapter 1 we outline the structure of the alienated world view, exploring briefly the perception that life in culture is a nightmare compounded of misery, self-deception, pointlessness, and mutual cruelty. Each participant feels his actions to be unreal and feels himself to be the unwilling participant in or victim of a macabre charade. At the same time, he recognizes his complicity in the mass drama and hates himself for it. This leaves him, nonetheless, with the dilemma of feeling unable to break free.

In Chapter 2 we relate this dramatized theme to the conflicts and pain suffered by ordinary people in their everyday existence. The feelings of unreality, victimization, pointlessness, and despair seem not to be the sole province of the alienated few nor of the artistic and intellectual elite. They are, as we hear them, feelings with which many of us must grapple. They continue to resurface, in myraid forms, regardless of how tenaciously we try to push them away. These attempts to bury feelings of alienation can mean denying them (an unconvincing insistence that one really does feel good) or, more usually, explaining the feeling away. This latter strategem often takes the form of an explanation: "If it weren't for [poverty, crime, middle-class greed, etc.], my life would be full." One's existence then becomes a crusade to obliterate the X, which, by its very nature, cannot be erased. Despair, in this frame of reference, is not experienced as fundamental to one's being. Indeed, one is always on the verge of overcoming his sense of misery. Paradoxically, the self, in this constellation, often expresses disbelief about this very proposition, often expresses the notion that it is lying to itself.

In Chapter 3 we focus on the struggles of two of literature's most compelling despairers: Herzog and Invisible Man. Each begins with the stance characterized in Chapter 2, and each embarks on a personal odyssey into his own being, into his alienation. In the process of this journey each man engages himself in a battle to divest himself of what he knows to be illusions. The journey's path is not straight, the alienated self continues to struggle with its proclivity to escape back into bad faith and clothe itself with a culturally defined identity. Each man ends his journey naked, daring to seek a free existence which feels more real, but without knowing if he will succeed or even what success will look like.

Under Part II, in Chapter 4, we reconsider one of Freud's case studies from a more existential-phenomenological perspective. We believe, as did Freud, that "patients" can serve to illuminate and underline common characteristics in human functioning. On the most universal level the cases demonstrate the processes by which men construct lives they subsequently experience as onerous and alien. The patients, like other despairers, feel oppressed by "reality." They see circumstances, the unfeelingness or malice of others, or even the will of God, as separating them from the possibility of feeling whole. At the same time they disbelieve their own explanations of themselves and the world. They "know"—that is, that they have created bogus realities that keep them trapped. Liberating themselves requires, first and foremost, a negation of their own beliefs. Experiencing an identity between the self and these basic readings of reality, the patient trembles at the very prospect of change. He is terrified of how he might experience himself shorn of his protective, self-serving explanations of his inner pain. Each patient, like Herzog and the Invisible Man, vacillates between experiencing himself as the agent of his own suffering and generating an inner picture of reality which exonerates him of all wrong doing. With this latter strategy he locks himself forever in an unreal existence. That is, he continues to experience his own bad faith and to recognize his own lies. Nonetheless, when locked in this position, he feels morally justified in attempting to destroy others. It is, after all, "they" who persecute him. Continual confusion over whether one is killer or victim is a hallmark of the bad faith posture, as is the inability to accept and experience inner pleasure and pain. These patients reveal how one can refuse to live one's life as himself. Madmen are not unique in their desires, nor even in their attempted strategy of living. What separates them from others is the nakedness of their conflict over their bad faith and the idiosyncratic forms they choose to express it. For most of us, culture provides common, shared formulas for living unreal lives in which we feel oppressed. The other men around us, in living similar lives and having similar beliefs, help to insulate us from experiencing alternatives or questioning our assumptions.

Yet such collective bad faith (collusion) is possible. By looking at how men live in societies very separate from our own, we can better recognize how people are able to reinforce their own and one another's commitment to utter "nonsense." This nonsense is not random, not a series of errors, but is designed to shield men from perceiving themselves and their own inner experiences.

Chapters 5 and 6 elaborate the formula of alienated existence as it is enacted on a collective level. In order to maintain their bad faith, their sense of being the helpless victims of reality, people collude to dramatize these perceptions. Through the medium of culture, they create definitions of self and other which lock them forever in positions where they feel both constrained and unreal. This basic characteristic of culture goes through enormous elaboration. Culture becomes both a protective force—shielding the self from its own strivings and from the evil intentions of the other—and at the same time an oppressive force to be resisted. If one is protected from the perils of existence by his own unreality, he also suffers from not being "allowed" to be real. Men rarely experience their own role in creating and maintaining the collusion. Instead, they feel as if culture is imposing their suspension in time upon them. To the degree that they know collective institutions and beliefs as unreal, men experience a sense of absurdity. They see themselves and others being "controlled" by myth, by chimeras. This can lead to diverse feelings and actions: disgust and capitulation, elation, or a sense of freedom from the paper tiger other men fear. Perceptions of the absurd are characteristic of all cultures and institutions, but tend to be fleeting experiences. That is, men see the absurd and feel momentarily disentangled from it, but then plunge back into bad faith as if the weight of culture cannot be resisted.

This ebbing and waning of the experience of the absurd, this movement back and forth between the self and some image one represents as the self, characterizes the experience of alienation. It can be seen as a central quality of despair, of madness, of the disquietude men feel in culture. Our epilogue summarizes what alienation expresses about this conflict and the tension it engenders. The longing to live openly and fully as one's self continues to press for change. It continually encounters the fear of this untested venture, a fear that drives one back to cultural prescriptions as a safe if painful refuge. The same issue that confronts the despairer now confronts us collectively: does the pain of living in bad faith outweigh our fear of seeking an alternative? If it does, shall we choose mutual self-destruction or shall we choose experimentation with new forms of living? There is, we would think, no way to predict the outcome of this conflict. Our choices are yet to be made.

References

1. William Barrett, *Irrational Man*, Garden City, L.I., Doubleday Anchor (1962).
2. Albert Camus, *The Rebel*, New York, Vintage Books (1956).
3. Bruce Jay Friedman, *The Dick*, New York, Bantam Books (1971).
4. Joachim Israel, *Alienation: From Marx to Modern Sociology*, Boston, Allyn and Bacon (1971).
5. Kenneth Kenniston, *The Uncommitted*, New York, Delta Books (1965).
6. Soren Kierkegaard, *The Sickness unto Death*, Princeton, N.J., Princeton University Press (1968).
7. Michael Novak, "The Social World of Individuals," *The Hastings Center Studies*, 2, No. 3 (Sept. 1974).
8. Richard Schacht, *Alienation*, Garden City, L.I., Doubleday (1970).

PART I
The Self's Struggle To Be Itself

1. A Culture of Discontent

Alienation represents one of the dominant themes in mass culture. In the novels of Heller and Vonnegut it surfaces as the perception of society absurd to the point of collective madness. In less sophisticated expressions, like the films "Serpico" or "Godfather," society is represented as so corrupt as to be nauseating and frightful. There is a group of such statements in contemporary culture which coalesces around a special mood, around a given image of reality. Such works present, in many ways, a common set of perceptions about the dilemma of the self in culture. They are, in this sense, a functioning culture of discontent. As a culture, as a way of looking at the world, these messages are peculiarly one-sided. Cultures have traditionally invoked images of what one "ought" to do, and have provided some prescription for action based on their world view. The culture of discontent is an anti-culture. It propounds a world view that any prescription for action is a bogus construct to be resisted. It therefore provides no answers, only skepticism toward collective rules. Nonetheless, some in our society have adopted this anti-culture as their own and have come to see the world in its terms. Others drift in and out of the culture of discontent, incorporating some aspects of it, discarding others. By no means is this culture obscure. Many of its leading documents have become major foci for the mass culture of the 1960's and early 70's. It may or may not express a prevailing consciousness, but it does present an intriguing set of images and perceptions. Exploring this expressive constellation may tell us something about alienation, and about the nature of human relationships.

If we approach the culture of discontent from this perspective, it can be seen both as expressing a view of the world and as the expression of a conflict. The world view is a particular interpretation and set of observations about social reality. Society, in this literature, is portrayed as a collusion or shared fantasy. Collective life thus becomes a kind of self-imposed nightmare which men propagate but then regard as "given" by the nature of external reality.

A feeling tone is clearly associated with this perspective, and is highly consonant in such diverse forms as black-humor fiction and radical psychiatry. Life is seen as a pointless, agonizing exercise. Billy Pilgrim, the everyman protagonist of Vonnegut's *Slaughterhouse Five*, comments on his experiences as an infantryman in World War II. There he witnessed the fire-bombing of Dresden. Billy recognizes this attack as one of the most brutal acts ever performed by civilized men, but simultaneously believes it to be the central experience of his life. It has, he believes, given him a mission: to bear witness to the bestiality of war by writing about the fire bombing and its aftermath. He ultimately becomes aware that he cannot use what he has seen to awaken mankind and alter history.

> I think of how useless the Dresden part of my memory
> has been, and yet how tempting Dresden has been to write
> about, and I am reminded of the famous limerick:
>
> > There was a young man from Stamboul,
> > Who soliloquized thus to his tool:
> > "You took all my wealth
> > And you ruined my health,
> > And now you won't pee, you old fool."
>
> And I'm reminded, too, of the song that goes:
>
> > My name is Yon Yonson,

> I work in Wisconsin,
> I work in a lumbermill there.
> The people I meet when I walk down the street,
> They say, "What's your name?"
> And I say,
> "My name is Yon Yonson,
> I work in Wisconsin . . ."

And so on to infinity. (9:2–3)

All the "transformations" and "dramatic moments" in Billy's life come to be seen as repetitions of Dresden. Their "significance" appears retrospectively to be no more than an illusion. Since his life and his conceptions of self have centered on these illusions, Billy's entire existence is portrayed as essentially a "nightmare of meaninglessness."

> And we were flown to a rest camp in France, where
> we were fed chocolate malted milkshakes and other rich
> foods until we were all covered with baby fat. Then we
> were sent home, and I married a pretty girl who was
> covered with baby fat too.
> And we had babies.
> And they're all grown up now, and I'm an old fart with
> his memories and his Pall Malls. My name is Yon Yonson,
> I work in Wisconsin, I work in a lumbermill there. (9:6)

In Vonnegut's elaborate tapestry there is a linkage between the pointlessness and absurdity of the voyage and the violence that surrounds it. His protagonists sense their own absence of purpose. They come to feel empty and vindictively cruel. It is as if violence represents their only means of being distracted from their inner torment. The fire bombing mission turns the landscape into a hell on earth: dead, barren, hollow, and lifeless. That is, the violence is used to externalize and represent the disastrous internal landscape of its perpetrators.

Laing, defining the stance of radical psychiatry and social criticism, echoes Vonnegut's perception. In the *Politics of Ex-*

perience he seems to be declaring a personal war on the tide of culture, throwing down the gauntlet: "The condition of alienation, of being asleep, of being out of one's mind, is the condition of normal man." This accusation or judgment, as we shall see, is one of the central tenets of the culture of discontent. Those who are are avowedly alienated from the collectivity see those existing within it as truly or profoundly alienated. To locate one's being in the matrix of collective fantasy is to be alienated from the potential to be fully human and fully alive. Those who define themselves through culture are alienated in the sense that they can never recognize how they suffer like the "young man from Stamboul." It is painful and disorienting to recognize the pointlessness of one's own existence. It is, on the other hand, absolutely deadening to live out one's pointlessness while maintaining the fiction that it is rewarding and inevitable. Maintaining this myth of self demands an almost total dissociation from feeling and is therefore untenable, leading only to internal anguish expressed in the cold murderousness evidenced in Dresden.

Although these principles appear to be regarded as absolute, they underlie a conflict that characterizes the entire culture of discontent. Even in the context of experiencing collective existence as a nightmare, the need to be grounded in the social world seems to remain. The feeling persists that the self cannot simply do without other human beings. One feels needful and deprived without human contact. Even when such isolation is foreborn, the self finds it almost impossible to be oblivious to the attempts of others to act upon him or on one another. The alienated self, like Billy, yearns to cry out against humanity. Simultaneously, the self is repelled by the very process of entering into the social world, even to the extent of denouncing it. The problem lies in the perception that dissent—calling to others to alter or abandon the collective fantasy—leads one to take part in the stylized drama. The "revolutionary" comes to perceive his self (and have it treated by others) as a kind of persona. To fight against culture one makes himself precisely what he is trying to escape from being: another object in the collusive fantasy. Thus the entrance into a social role is seen as the only available modality for human contact. At the same time, occupying such a role is experienced as a negation of self, a fraudulent act.

As we elaborate these themes, most readers will recognize their tremendous redundancy on the cultural scene. The "black humor" genre in novels and films, many of the most popular rock composers, the living theater, and other trends in experimental dramatic forms, to take some obvious examples, seem to revolve around the problem of how to express and explore the fundamental assumptions we have just sketched. We will build the current discussion around three primary documents: Kurt Vonnegut's *Sirens of Titan* (first published in 1959 but "discovered" in the 1960's) and the autobiographical writings of Eldridge Cleaver (*Soul on Ice*) and Abbie Hoffman (*Revolution for the Hell of It*). These works represent an expression of the "culture of discontent" at a time when it was most aggressively outspoken and revolutionary in its tone. They allow us to see most clearly these fundamental assumptions as expressed in different forms.

The perceptions common to the culture of discontent are linked to a vision or image of society. Vonnegut's world view, which is remarkably consistent throughout his writing, covers many of the major elements in the alienated world view. *Sirens*, one of his earliest novels, is a black-humor science-fiction fantasy. One major protagonist, Winston Niles Rumfoord, is a New England patrician who has mastered travel through time and space. He cannot, unfortunately, determine his own movements, materializing and dematerializing at different places in a pattern that is out of his control. Using this ability (or affliction) and the resources it indirectly puts into his hands, Rumfoord begins meddling with earth's history. In this process, he "causes" enormous suffering and upheavals. Vonnegut makes it clear that his actions are impelled by ennui, boredom, and the gnawing emptiness associated with his own physical impotence, which is a symbol of the deadness and self-loathing Rumfoord is impelled to share with others. He finds in mankind a receptive audience. The suffering and self estrangement he inflicts always has its basis in the "victim's" own corruption. Rumfoord provides the stimulus for new and deadly collusions, essentially no madder than the fantasies his recruits are living out before he finds them. The alienated quality of the novel is enhanced by the "detachment" the reader comes to share with Rumfoord. The activity of Earthlings is seen as if from afar. They become specimens under a microscope, more quaint than real. Through this lens of detachment, we are called upon to shrug at the fact that their lives represent a kind of absurd macabre drama.

> The Earthlings behaved at all times as though there were a big eye in the sky—as though that big eye were ravenous for entertainment.
> The big eye was a glutton for great theater. The big eye was indifferent as to whether the Earthling shows were comedy, tragedy, farce, satire, athletics, or vaudeville. Its demand, which Earthlings apparently found as irresistible as gravity, was that the shows be great.
> The demand was so powerful that Earthlings did almost nothing but perform for it, night and day—and even in their dreams. (8:276)

"The Band," one of the most well known rock groups of the late sixties and early seventies, attempts to express precisely this same vision of social reality as a collusive fantasy. Their fourth album—appropriately enough entitled "Cahoots" —begins with the composition "Life is a Carnival."

> Saw a man with the jinx—in the third degree
> From trying to deal with people—people you can't see
> Take away—take away—this house of mirrors
> Give away—give away—all the souvenirs

We're all in the same boat ready to float off the edge
  of the world
This flat old world
The street is a sideshow from the peddler to the corner girl
Life is a carnival—it's in the book
Life is a carnival—take another look.

In both metaphors, "people" are no more than imagos desperately acting out pseudo-realities. The desperation and misery of the actors are the only indicators of a possible counter-reality, the only basis for believing that the imagos are or can be anything more than puppets playing out an arbitrary script. The alienated commentator seems, in the most extreme instances, to doubt even the potential humanity of the cultural players. Like Vonnegut's protagonist, he can begin to experience himself as a kind of lone possessor of subjectivity: "Unk had the eerie feeling that he and Boaz were the only real people in the stone building—that the rest were glass-eyed robots, and not very well made robots at that" (8:112).

In some instances the culture of discontent sees the presentation of the drama as an attempt to fill up internal and existential emptiness. Alternatively, the carnival or the "show" for the "big eye" are also portrayed as concealing devices. The show can be a means of pushing away feelings and realities that would force the actors to look inside themselves and become something other than imagos. In Vonnegut's writing, two major characteristics of the drama are that it is without purpose, and that all the players—no matter how "good" or "bad" their parts (that is, no matter what their place in social hierarchy)—find participation intolerable.

Evangelist Bobby Denton's image of Earth as God's
space ship was an apt one—particularly with reference to
barflies. Helmholtz and Miss Wiley were behaving like pilot
and co-pilot of an enormously pointless voyage through
space that was expected to take forever. It was easy to believe that they had begun the voyage nattily, flushed with

youth and technical training, and that the bottles before them were the instruments they had been watching for years and years and years.

It was easy to believe that each day had found the space boy and the space girl microscopically more slovenly than the day before, until now, when they were the shame of the Pan-Galactic Space Service.

Two buttons on Helmholtz's fly were open. There was shaving cream in his left ear. His socks did not match.

Miss Wiley was a crazy-looking little old lady with a lantern jaw. She wore a frizzy black wig that looked as though it had been nailed to a farmer's barn door for years. (8:87)

Participation in the fantasy of culture leads only to a continual degradation or debasement of self. One takes a part in the collective drama primed for accomplishment, primed for a transformation or birth of "self." Instead, the actor is rewarded with the experience of himself as shoddy, corrupt, deteriorating without moving anywhere.

It is also somewhat remarkable how this particular perception dovetails with observations made from the other side of the cultural fence—that is, observations by certain "straight" social scientists. Erving Goffman, for example, in his classic and influential *Presentation of Self in Everyday Life* (1959), also employs a dramaturgic metaphor in describing collective behavior. The activity of being "in" culture is dealt with essentially as a performance whereby the actor consciously and unconsciously works toward the goal of "impression management." He attempts to foist on the audience an image of his self which he knows to be incomplete, inaccurate or totally fallacious. One can never "be" all those things he is supposed to be in order to have a moral right to the role he is making claim upon. Though each actor experiences himself and his activities as fraudulent, he somehow manages to think of the overall structure of the drama as real, and to be continually crushed when he attempts movement, only to find himself in another sector of fraudulence.

It is interesting to note that while each team will be in a position to appreciate the unsavory "unperformed" aspects of its own backstage behavior, it is not likely to be in a position to come to a similar conclusion about the teams with which it interacts. When pupils leave the schoolroom and go outside for a recess of familiarity and misconduct, they often fail to appreciate that their teachers have retired to a "common room" to swear and smoke in a similar recess of backstage behavior. We know, of course, that a team with only one member can take a very dark view of itself and that not a few psychotherapists find employment in alleviating this guilt, making their living by telling individuals the facts of other people's lives. Behind these realizations about oneself and illusions about others is one of the important dynamics and disappointments of social mobility, be it mobility upward, downward, or sideways. In attempting to escape from a two-faced world of front region and back region behavior, individuals may feel that in the new position they are attempting to acquire they will be the character projected by individuals in that position and not at the same time a performer. When they arrive, of course, they find their new situation has unanticipated similarities with their old one; both involve a presentation of front to an audience and both involve the presenter in the grubby, gossipy business of staging a show. (5:132–33)

Social mobility, then, or any form of "striving" as defined by culture, leads only to confrontation with one's own fantasies. Striving, adaptation, and conformity are pursued on the basis of faith: faith that "becoming" some other persona in culture will make one feel alive and whole. Vonnegut continually hammers at the absurdity of this belief.

A secondary character in *Sirens* is Ransom K. Fern, financial manager of the world's richest estate. Incredibly wealthy in his own right, he provides us with an evaluation of existence in culture which is the basis of his shrewdness.

Ransom K. Fern turned away from the window. His face was a troubling combination of youth and age. There was no sign in the face of any intermediate stages in the aging process, no hint of the man of thirty or forty or fifty who had been left behind. Only adolescence and the age of sixty were represented. It was as though a seventeen-year-old had been withered and bleached by a blast of heat.

Fern read two books a day. It has been said that Aristotle was the last man to be familiar with the whole of his own culture. Ransom K. Fern had made an impressive attempt to equal Aristotle's achievement. He had been somewhat less successful than Aristotle in perceiving patterns in what he knew.

The intellectual mountain had labored to produce a philosophical mouse—and Fern was the first to admit that it was a mouse, and a mangy mouse at that. As Fern expressed the philosophy conversationally, in its simplest terms:

"You go up to a man, and you say, 'How are things going, Joe?' And he says, 'Oh, fine, fine—couldn't be better.' And you look into his eyes, and you see things really coudn't be much worse. When you get right down to it, everybody's having a perfectly lousy time of it, and I mean everybody. And the hell of it is, nothing seems to help much."

This philosophy did not sadden him. It did not make him brood.

It made him fearlessly watchful.

It helped in business, too—for it let Fern assume automatically that the other fellow was far weaker and far more bored than he seemed.

Sometimes, too, people with strong stomachs found Fern's murmured asides funny. (8:68–69)

The combination of pointlessness and misery comes together for the individual in a sense of living death, in occupying space that is an endless purgatory. It is this suspension in misery, denied and evaded but always lurking behind the eyes, which Kierkegaard called the "sickness unto death." It is this sickness which Laing diagnoses as characterizing those defining themselves through culture. Vonnegut can only show us his perception of it through the medium of black humor. By emphasizing the absurdity rather than the painfulness of the big show, he makes it possible to laugh at one's own misery.

Fern's original employer is the world's richest man, Noel Constant. Despite his wealth, he lives in a single furnished room in a beaten up hotel. Noel's fortune began when he was inspired to use the Bible as his financial guide. His program is to take the first two letters of the Bible and purchase the first stock having those initials on the New York Stock Exchange. Each day thereafter, once the value of the initial stock had doubled, he would put his entire fortune on the stock designated by the next two letters. No one, of course, is privy to this secret, and Noel is attributed with acumen bordering on omniscience. He remains essentially uninvolved and unchanged by his "success." Avoiding human contact, he begets a son by impregnating the chambermaid, "who spent one night in ten with him for a small flat fee" (8:75). He refuses contact with the son, Malachi, but retains the mother's services and provides for them both. Having seen the son on his twenty-first birthday, he provides him with the secret of increasing the family estate, by leaving him a brief note of explanation upon his death.

> If I wasn't a very good father or a very good anything that was because I was as good as dead for a long time before I died. Nobody loved me and I wasn't very good at anything and I couldn't find any hobbies I liked and I was sick and tired of selling pots and pans and watching television so I was as good as dead and I was too far gone to ever come back. (8:90–91)

There is nothing that one can "achieve" to relieve the oppression of being suspended in time. There is also no gift that can elevate one's existence beyond a sickness unto death. Malachi inherits his father's wealth and becomes the world's richest man. Although totally dedicated to his own pleasure, his life remains a slimy misery.

> Malachi Constant lay in the wide gutter of his kidney-shaped swimming pool, sleeping the sleep of a drunkard. There was a quarter of an inch of warm water in the gutter. Constant was fully dressed in blue-green evening shorts and a dinner jacket of gold brocade. His clothes were soaked.
>
> He was all alone.
>
> The pool had once been covered uniformly by an undulating blanket of gardenias. But a persistent morning breeze had moved the blooms to the foot of a bed. In folding back the blanket, the breeze revealed a pool bottom paved with broken glass, cherries, twists of lemon peel, peyotl buttons, slices of orange, stuffed olives, sour onions, a television set, a hypodermic syringe, and the ruins of a white grand piano. Cigar butts and cigarette butts, some of them marijuana, littered the surface.
>
> The swimming pool looked less like a facility for sport than like a punchbowl in hell. (8:53)

Vonnegut systematically ravishes our prevalent myths of transformation. Collective belief describes and defines given acts, possessions, states of being as both morally uplifting and ecstatic. We define these products as scarce, as the privileges granted by society to those who "achieve." The shared assumption is that if one were in a different place in this hierarchy, he would somehow feel good. We accept as reasonable the fact that we currently feel rotten, insubstantial, and impotent: these experiences of self would dissipate if culture stopped depriving us of the goods we need to feel complete. In this feeling of incompleteness each player feels unable to begin living. Since "others" have robbed the self of the very opportunity to begin living, the actor feels morally justified and even impelled to seize back that opportunity. The modality of this seizure is theft. Man in culture is continually enacting a paranoid plot. In his experience of being he must rip off others in order to survive, in order to begin "living." The culture of discontent, with both glee and sadness, dwells on the absurdity of these assumptions. If mainstream culture is dominated by the image of a social hierarchy that one climbs to enhance the sense of well being, much of the alienated literature focuses on the self-delusive quality of the metaphor. Movement up or down the ladder is seen as no more than the trading of one form of misery for another: hunger for pointlessness, moral outrage for the sense of emptiness.

One of Bob Dylan's best known songs, "When I Paint My Masterpiece," reinforces Vonnegut's basic image:

Train-wheels runnin' through the back of my memory,
When I ran on the hilltop followin' a pack of wild geese
Someday, everything is gonna sound like a rhapsody,
When I paint my masterpiece
Sailin' round the world in a dirty gondola,
Oh to be back in the land of Coca-Cola

The self-mocking quality of the image really has two cutting edges. First is the juxtaposition between the fantasy or illusion of the transformed self and the mundane, sleazy, absurd quality of all that is observable. If everything in one's own existence is insubstantial—indeed, a parody of itself—the self can still expect to leap forward to another plane of being where idyllic fantasy and reality will coalesce. The second level of the counterpoint is the authors' self-acknowledged inability to accept the consequences of their perception. The agony of their alienation is that it does not release them from the absurdity of their own behavior. Climbing the social hierarchy confronts the self with the delusive quality of his expectations. In the subsequent alienation, despair becomes deeper. Not only does one still feel incomplete, but he can no longer even believe that he knows how to become whole. This leads to panic and dread. In alienation one can feel fraudulent and insubstantial and no longer believe that things will magically "get better." The Band comments on its own plight:

> Now deep in the heart of a lonely kid,
> who suff'red so much for what he did
> they gave this ploughboy his fortune and fame
> since that day he ain't been the same.
>
> See the man with the Stage Fright,
> Just standin' up there t' give it all his might,
> and he got caught in the spotlight
> when we get to the end
> he wants t' start all over again.
>
> I've got fire water right on my breath,
> and the doctor warned me I might catch a death
> said, "you can make it in your disguise,
> Just never show the fear that's in your eyes."

Those within culture are portrayed as working constantly to stave off these perceptions, to ward off the experience of alienation which threatens to intrude upon them. The feelings of dread and emptiness are counteracted by pointless activity and paranoia. These are prevailing characteristics of mad drama represented by culture. The dynamic unfolded in Vonnegut's image is that people enter into the absurd drama to foreclose choice, to shut out truth and to escape themselves. Bee, one of the protagonists, comments on the experience of being used as an automaton in a self-consciously suicidal plot to attack earth from Mars.

> "The mighty Rumfoord—" said Bee.
> "Pardon me?" said Brackman.
> "He snatched us out of our lives," said Bee. "He put us to sleep. He cleaned out our minds the way you clean the seeds out of a jack-o'-lantern. He wired us like robots,

trained us, aimed us—burned us out in a good cause." She shrugged.

"Could we have done any better if he'd left us in charge of our own lives?" said Bee. "Would we have become any more—or any less? I guess I'm glad he used me. I guess he had a lot better ideas about what to do with me than Florence White or Darlene Simpkins or whoever I was.

"But I hate him all the same," said Bee.

"That's your privilege," said Brackman. "He said that was the privilege of every Martian."

"There's one consolation," said Bee. "We're all used up. We'll never be of any use to him again." (8:242)

Once again, we see the conflict or curious double perception of the actress. She "knows" that she is willing to be "used," and was a willing accomplice in the act of her utilization. At the same time, she can hate the other for having used her, and reassure herself that vigilance is no longer required. Without any evidence, Bee decides that she is exempt from involvement in future plots. In fact, her role in the absurd drama is just beginning, and becomes more central and more insane as the story evolves. To the extent that she no longer even bothers to be wary, she has helped to ensure her renewed recruitment into Rumfoord's plot. We can see the utility of this for Bee. The sense of being a victim in an alien plot, rather than the author of one's own pointlessness, is both an outlet and a self-justification. The hatred of the manipulator sustains the actor. Self-hatred need not be confronted when one is occupied in the struggle against some tyrant. In this sense the moral pose of victim seems to predominate for those in the drama. The actor remains "innocent" of the deeds he performs. He experiences himself as the prisoner of the script, which is backed by the overwhelming weight of external "reality."

Vonnegut represents this sense of personal helplessness in the metaphor of "the Army of Mars." Each soldier has had an antenna placed in his skull. This antenna forces compliance to all commands, and induces excruciating pain in anyone who resists or even questions the absurdity of the enterprise. The soldiers of the Army of Mars—all recruited from earth—reflect the prevailing stance toward social control. They regard the antenna as natural, as having nothing to do with the volitional acts of men. Concomitantly, each feels obliged to adapt, to limit the parameters of his being to those which the antenna will accept.

Malachi, renamed Unk when serving in the Army of Mars, makes an effort at remembering his former existence. He performs this forbidden act at the urging of Boaz, a secret "commander" of the Army of Mars. Boaz then rewards his efforts by activating Unk's antenna with a hidden device.

> When Unk came to on the barrack floor, his buddy Boaz was daubing Unk's temples with a cold washrag.
>
> Unk's squadmates stood in a circle around Unk and Boaz. The faces of the squadmates were unsurprised, unsympathetic. Their attitude was that Unk had done something stupid and unsoldierly, and so deserved what he got.
>
> They looked as though Unk had done something as militarily stupid as silhouetting himself against the sky or cleaning a loaded weapon, as sneezing on patrol or contracting and not reporting a venereal disease, as refusing a direct order or sleeping through reveille, as being drunk on guard or drawing to an inside straight, as keeping a book or a live hand grenade in his footlocker, as asking who had started the Army anyway and why . . . (8:113)

Most men are seen as content, like Bee, to turn themselves into robots, instruments of an external and incomprehensible plan. The plan itself is always absurd. Men utilize one another in their personal dramas only to be used in turn. The feeling of misery and unfulfillment is characteristic of both positions. The drama Malachi stages is the rape of Bee. He attacks her in the dark so that his victim lacks human identity. "It was a joyless union, satisfactory to no one but Mother Nature at her most callous" (8:161). Discovering who his victim is, he is overwhelmed by his brutishness. At this point Malachi "realized for the first time what most people never realize about themselves—that he was not only a victim of outrageous fortune, but one of outrageous fortune's cruelest agents as well" (8:162).

The only alternative to this bleak misery is resistance to the collective drama. Resisting requires the willingness to fight through pain. Malachi's friend, Stony, is eventually executed for perceiving too clearly the madness of the Army of Mars. He leaves behind a note: "Almost everything I know for sure has come from fighting the pain. Whenever I start to turn and look at something, and the pain comes, I keep turning my head anyway [in order to] see something I'm not supposed to see" (8:125). Even in the absence of a positive goal or alternative, Vonnegut's characters continue to struggle, to grope for some existential premise outside of the myth. This liberation of self is associated with awakening, and sometimes even with elation. Boaz is wrenched from this position as a "True Commander" of the Martian Army, and for the first time realizes that he has been no more than a puppet manipulating other puppets. He controlled men through their antennae but never really understood the function of his command. He had only followed a script laid down by Rumfoord, never asking himself why. He reacts to this perception by

> laughing at the ferocious mess he was in—at the way he had pretended all his army life that he had understood everything that was going on, and that everything that was going on was just fine.
>
> He was laughing at the dumb way he had let himself be used—by God knows who for God knows what. (8:182–83)

However, this movement out of a given myth system is ambivalent. The protagonists do little more than seek some other form of self delusion which will sustain them. The actor wishes to be free of the drama but cannot confront his own reality and the meaning of his own acts. As they struggle after being stranded on Mercury, Boaz and Unk (Malachi) each attempts to find a way to live, and some purchase on his past. Unk is disturbed by the way Boaz attempts to find a structure for his existence. Boaz has temporarily found a kind of contentment playing "God Almighty" to the harmoniums of Mercury, a species of unisex, identical creatures to which

> [h]unger, envy, ambition, fear, indignation, religion and sexual lust are irrelevant and unknown. The creatures have only one sense: touch [and] have only two possible messages. The first is an automatic response to the second, and the second is an automatic response to the first.
>
> The first is, "Here I am, here I am, here I am."
>
> The second is, "So glad you are, so glad you are, so glad you are." (8:186)

Since the harmoniums live on vibration, Boaz is a magnet to them. His pulse and heartbeat are irresistible attractions, and he even plays music to transport the creatures to ecstasy. Unk becomes infuriated by Boaz's attributing character and intent to the harmoniums, and tries to point out Boaz's "madness" in dealing with them. At the same time, Boaz knows the one secret that would destroy Unk's sustaining illusion: "Unk was living on dreams of a reunion with Stony." In fact, Unk had served as Stony's executioner on Mars, strangling him as instructed through his antenna. Unk does not know the identity of his victim and thinks Stony to be still alive. As Unk tries to make Boaz "face reality," Boaz develops his own response.

> "Don't *truth* me," said Boaz in his thoughts, "and I won't *truth* you." It was a plea he had made several times to Unk.
>
> Boaz had invented the plea, and its meaning was this: Unk was to stop telling Boaz truths about the harmoniums, because Boaz loved the harmoniums, and because Boaz was nice enough not to bring up truths that would make Unk unhappy. (8:202–203)

Unk, like Vonnegut's other characters, can only reenter his own fantasies. There is a mild sense in which these seem preferable to the collective fantasies that preceded them. They are benign, involving no need to hurt others. The personal fantasy is nonetheless self-delusion. It is based on a denial of what one knows to be true about himself. As such, the fantasies that Vonnegut's wanderers seek to hide in are not so much convincing as ludicrous. Salo, the intergalactic traveler, sums up this view of destiny: "Anybody who has traveled this far on a fool's errand has no choice but to uphold the honor of fools by completing the errand" (8:313). Absurdity becomes aware of itself in a context of helpless (if sardonic) resignation.

The black humor metaphors, although tending toward the hysterical, contain the seeds of a serious set of perceptions. The self in culture can indeed feel that the social world is dangerously mad. The struggle to move out of the collective fantasy, out of the murderous scenario of his culture, is the consuming struggle for Eldridge Cleaver in *Soul on Ice*. The particular myth that enshrouds him is white racism. Those fighting to be free of inner and outer constraints of racist society "experience this system of social control as madness." The continuity with Vonnegut and Laing's metaphor of society as nightmare is striking. As Cleaver describes it, his initial understanding of white racism (and his own relation to it) was associated with a sense of "awakening." It also evoked fundamental rage, both to be free and to destroy. In stripping away the façade of reality represented by culture, Cleaver must suffer the pain of confronting his own fantasy structure.

> It became clear that it was possible for me to take the initiative: intead of simply *reacting* I could *act* . . . My mind would be free and no power in the universe could force me to accept something if I didn't want to . . .
>
> This little game got good to me and I got good at it. I attacked all forms of piety, loyalty, and sentiment: marriage, love, God, patriotism, the Constitution, the founding fathers, law, concepts of right-wrong-good-evil, all forms of

ritualized and conventional behavior. As I pranced about, club in hand, seeking new idols to smash, I encountered really for the first time in my life, with any seriousness, The Ogre, rising up before me in a mist. I discovered, with alarm, that The Ogre possessed a tremendous and dreadful power over me . . . I, a black man, confronted The Ogre— the white woman. (1:19–20)

Cleaver experiences guilt and rage at self for his overwhelming lust for white women. He experiences this affliction as coming from his designated place in the white myth structure. In his attachment to this ogre, Cleaver sees that he is living as the very imago attributed to the black in the white myth structure. He also recognizes that his driven, hateful desire represents a negation of himself as a black. It testifies to the feeling that Cleaver, as a black man, longs for completion through finding his antithesis. We can see this as a particular case of Vonnegut's formula. Each man pursues that which he is not and cannot be in the belief that this pursuit will make him feel whole.

Indeed, this state of incompleteness—and eternal separation from that which can make the self feel alive—is characteristic of each imago in the racial mythology.

There is a fundamental fractionation of self, or psychological division of labor, in the system. Each individual is kept in a state of limbo where he does not and cannot experience himself as totally human. In this schema, the black man must wear the persona of the "supermasculine menial." He has physical strength and virility, but the labor his strength produces is harnessed to the white man's ends. His virility remains mere potentiality, since the white man controls access to the valued sexual objects. The black man becomes an ambivalent image of castrated and controlled potency. The other major personas in the collective drama are likewise only permitted to be partially alive. Each must live in the state of feeling incomplete and being barred from the object that will give it a sense of

36

wholeness; the reciprocal for each becomes its taboo. Each must also despise itself while ambivalently, secretly, reveling in that which it has. Each occupant of an imago is unwilling to let go and have the fantasy constructs of the system collapse. Like Laing's schizoids, they would seemingly rather remain in their safe prison, which is oppressively painful, than try to liberate the self.

In Cleaver's analysis, the black male becomes the emotive focal point of the entire myth structure. He is incomplete in that he cannot acquire that which the myth has assigned to the white man. The black man is defined as unable to have intellectual mastery, social power, or control over the environment or himself. Nor can he possess the white woman, whom he is compelled to covet. The black woman is available to him but, on some fundamental level, is undesirable. Cleaver's symbolic prototype, "Old Lazarus," comments:

> There is no love left between a black man and a black woman. I love white women and hate black women. It's just me, so deep that I don't even try to get it out of me any more. I'd jump over ten nigger bitches just to get to one white woman. Ain't no such thing as an ugly white woman. A white woman is beautiful even if she's bald-headed and only has one tooth . . . (1:148)

The white woman is not "beautiful" because she represents sexual fulfillment. She is irresistible because she symbolizes the possibility of becoming a whole man, one who can act for himself. Everything of which the black man has been historically and psychologically deprived is dangled before him, personified in this taboo object: "I know that the white man made the black woman the symbol of slavery and the white woman the symbol of freedom. Every time I embrace a black woman I'm embracing slavery, and when I put my arms around a white woman, well, I'm hugging freedom" (1:149).

The white man, as the major perpetrator of the system of

mutual denigration, becomes the omnipotent administrator. He gives up his potency, and even the sense of being grounded in his own body, for a sense of disembodied control. Having transformed his experience of self into that of a machine or robot, he consequently must substitute the pornography of violence for his abrogated sexuality. For every quality that he attributes to himself in this crude, stereotypical way, he must disown the possibility of its opposite. To be rigidly controlled, the omnipotent administrator gives up his capacity for spontaneity and feeling. If he is to exert force through the elaborate machinery of social institutions and technology, he concomitantly experiences a lack of his own physical powers as opposed to the black lower classes.

This cycle of projective attribution must lead inevitably to the destruction of all. The more the administrator projects on the menial, the more he must create distance and rigid lines between "himself" and a black lower class. Everything associated with life and spontaneity becomes increasingly the "not-me." As the white man's existence becomes progressively impoverished, the projective totem (black man) becomes more and more an object of fear and hatred. The administrator must destroy him in order to get back all that he has projected. He can become obsessed with the project of castrating the blacks. Should he activate this desire, the white man would also destroy his own imago-self. The omnipotent administrator can't tolerate having his sexuality and aggression reside in the self. Without some external imago like that of the supermasculine menial, the omnipotent administrator cannot exist.

Similarly, white and black women are locked into separate, absurd personas that deny the possibility of life. The white woman yearns for some equivalent of the supermasculine menial to liberate her, while the black woman yearns to erase her blackness through being reborn as a white child. Each mythic role is thus engaged in an eternal struggle to complete the self. Each struggle is doomed to failure, since it represents the self seeking fulfillment through its own negation. In desperation people hack at and seek to destroy the mannequins playing opposite them, hoping thereby to seize the opportunity to live.

Regardless of Cleaver's perception of the metaphors underlying social "reality," he exhibits the same conflict as Vonnegut's characters. On the one hand, he wishes to disengage entirely from the myth structure. He seeks to stand on his own as a man, neither to be the role the myth would assign to him nor to live his life in reaction to these absurd attributions. This alternative is sought through direct, nonstereotyped human confrontation:

> Getting to know someone, entering that new world, is an ultimate, irretrievable leap into the unknown. The prospect is terrifying. The stakes are high. The emotions are overwhelming. The two people are reluctant really to strip themselves naked in front of each other, because in doing so they make themselves vulnerable and give enormous power over themselves one to the other . . .
>
> But I do not believe . . . that we have to be fraudulent and pretentious with one another. If we project fraudulent, pretentious images, or if we fantasize each other into distorted caricatures of what we really are, then, when we awake from the trance and see beyond the sham and front, all will dissolve, all will die or be transformed into bitterness and hate. (1:33–34)

It would thus appear that Cleaver "knows" the path he must take in the search for his own humanity. To take this path requires ignoring the collective, institutional world and seeking to relate to other human beings as himself ignoring both his own and their "social identities."

On the other hand, he feels the need to take on the fight within the drama as real. The destruction of racism and the racist are seen as preconditions for beginning to live. Cleaver must vacillate between the attempt to act as himself and his presentation as "black revolutionary." In a sense the very core of his being is the revolutionary struggle, a struggle that can be as integral and sustaining to the drama as the racist myth itself. Moreover, it demands from him a hatred, rage, and self-insulation which subvert the fearful search for his own humanity.

Abbie Hoffman is even more overtly trapped in the same paradox. Describing himself as a "revolutionary artist," he centers his activities on fighting an evil, collective fantasy. "The problem is not what to do in the revolution but what to do between the revolution" (4:186). Nowhere was the paradox of his anticultural stance more apparent than during his appearance on the Johnny Carson show. In a genial sense he played a clown in the circus he so loathed. Hoffman's expression of self is dependent on having something external to attack, something which can be destroyed without provoking guilt. "How can you define joy . . . joy is picking flowers in the woods. Joy is punching a cop when he steps on your toe . . . Joy is saying no and doing no to a government grown old and evil" (4:111).

The basic thrust of his book, however, is to underline the unreality of collective institutions. Once again we see culture as a myth created to account for and deal with our own behavior. The myth is that we can experience ourselves as innocent because we are like the Army of Mars, under external controls.

> There are no rules, only images . . . Eichmann lives by the rules. Eichmann, machinelike, twitching nervously, pushes at his steel-rimmed glasses, takes his neatly folded handkerchief from the breast pocket of his gray-flannel suit and mops his sweating bald forehead (An electrical engineer: *"My goal in life is to make myself replaceable"*—DOT-DOT-BEEP-BEEP).
>
> "My God was a pink memo. . . . I was a careerist (slow) I was only doing my death." (4:111)

Many of the incidents in Hoffman's narrative are no more

than tests and demonstrations of his perception that interaction is projective and mythic. He sees men in culture creating fantastic meanings out of the other's role but then acting as if that meaning were there and they are simply "perceiving" it. In talking about the effectiveness of the "diggers"—whose presentation he sees as guerrilla theater—Hoffman writes of how the ambiguity of their self-definition fed into this mad process of attribution based on nothing but the internal fears and fantasies of the observers.

> We become communist-racist-acid-headed freaks, holding flowers in one hand and bombs in the other. The Old Left says we work for the CIA. Ex-Marines stomp on us as Pinkos. Newport police jail us as smut peddlers. Newark cops arrest us as riot inciters. (These four events were all triggered by passing out free copies of the same poem.) (4:27)

A disturbing thing about Abbie Hoffman (and he enraged a great many people) was his ability to demonstrate the literal madness underlying everyday activity. Those living within and worshipping institutions become entrapped in mythic symbols and stereotyped responses. They become the slaves of their own artifacts, of the fantasies they have concretized.

Hoffman "demonstrates" at the Pentagon:

> FLASHBACK: Baby and I, complete with Uncle Sam hats and Flower Flags, jump a barbed-wire fence and are quickly surrounded by marshals and soldiers.
> "We're Mr. and Mrs. America, and we claim this land in the name of Free America."
> We plant the Flag and hold our ground. The troops are really shook. Do you club Uncle Sam? We're screaming incantations.
> "You're under arrest. What's your name?"
> "Mr. and Mrs. America, and Mrs. America's pregnant."

The troops lower their clubs in respect. A marshal writes in his book: "Mr. and Mrs. America—Trespassing." (4:42–43)

One can become "freed" from living out such enactments only by unilateral declaration. The act of recognizing the collective as fantastic creates for the individual the sense of possibility. Reality is not approached through altering social structures, but by disregarding them. A "digger" represents the prototype. "He sat on the stage with a flute in one hand and a tire iron in the other hand, drawing an imaginary circle around himself. 'I declare this area a liberated one. Anyone enters and I'll kill him'" (4:39).

The culture of discontent strives to present us with a possibility represented in the metaphor of this digger. Very simply, it invokes the notion of alternative modes of experiencing the self and the world. To seek these modes, each man must disengage from the fantasy called culture. This literature surely challenges our traditional equation between alienation and pathology. Alienation becomes, in fact, a first step in breaking loose from a collective, pervasive madness. Alienation is also seen as carrying with it a burden of fear, loneliness, and self-doubt.

References

1. Eldridge Cleaver, *Soul on Ice,* New York, Dell Publishing (1970).
2. R. L. Danko, L. Helm, and J. R. Robertson, "Life is a Carnival."
3. B. Dylan, "When I Paint My Masterpiece."
4. Free [Abbie Hoffman], *Revolution for the Hell of It*, New York, Dial Press (1968).
5. E. Goffman, *The Presentation of Self in Everyday Life,* Garden City, L.I., Anchor Books (1959).

6. R. D. Laing, *The Politics of Experience*, New York, Ballantine (1968)
7. Robbie Robertson, "Stage Fright," New York, Canaan Music (1970).
8. Kurt Vonnegut, *The Sirens of Titan*, New York, Dell (1959).
9. Kurt Vonnegut, *Slaughterhouse Five*, New York, Dell (1969).

2. In Search of the Experience of Self

The experience of alienation can no longer be considered the exclusive property of the artist or the outsider. The sense of dis-ease with the self and with culture has filtered into the everyday lives of ordinary people. Robert Coles, a Harvard-based psychiatrist and psychoanalyst, has spent much of his career doing depth interviews in sectors of the American public. Some of his best known and most highly respected studies have focused on deprived populations in the Deep South and in Appalachia. In the 1960's he was engaged in an intensive longitudinal study of ordinary people. The so-called middle Americans he interviewed were the schoolteachers, skilled craftsmen, and small businessmen who represent the majority of our population. He conveys his findings in a series of written portraits. In examining them the reader is exposed to the concerns, conflicts, self-perceptions, and world views which Coles has so skillfully elicited.

One of his general findings is that middle Americans feel very much embattled and resentful. They repeatedly assert that "for the workingman, the average guy, it's no picnic. Life, it's tough" (2:4). One of Cole's interviewees describes himself as struggling to keep his head "up over the water" (2:5) through constant effort, through putting in "slave time." This pursuit makes him feel "like a nigger . . . I'm back at work after supper, and I'll be sweating . . . and I'll say to myself: Joe you're a goddam slave, that's what you are; you might as well be picking cotton" (2:5).

This experience of bondage and pointlessness does not grow out of material deprivation. Joe tells us that he gets a "good salary," that he lives in a nice home, and that he really lives "as comfortably as anyone could ever want" (2:5). Like the radicals he finds so abhorrent and incomprehensible, Joe feels drawn to the notion of repudiating his ties to culture. He harbors an image of setting himself free. Joe and his wife feel anguish about the treadmill they are on: working on a hated job in which he feels like a slave in order to purchase things that bring little pleasure. He feels that "we've got to stop buying everything. Once I said we're going into the woods and live in a tent and hunt for food and grow it. She said that was fine with her . . . So I laughed; and she did, too" (2:5). The middle Americans, these ordinary people, as we shall see, have generated their own explanation of what is wrong with culture. Such explanations are not so very different from those held, for example, by social scientists, who have generally attempted to locate the source of unease in some institutional pattern gone awry, or in some erroneous cultural belief. The burden has been alternatively placed on child-rearing practices (1:47–48), the rate of social change, the burdens of affluence (5:273–79), and the decline of the extended family (4:Ch. 10). These "explanations" tend to reflect the more general theme that the root of the problem of alienation lies in the loss of something, such as religious values—something the people can believe in. As Philip Rieff has argued, old beliefs are dead, dissolved by the weight of history. We can no longer muster commitment to act out such mythic ideals as "economic man" or "religious man" (6:Ch. 1). In the past these prototypes served as a vehicle for shaping men's lives, for giving them a sense of purpose. Having lost belief in these ideals, we have been thrown back upon ourselves. We are currently without an adequate image for uniting men into a community and giving them some sense of inner peace.

Such explanations really do no more than enjoin us to re-establish our faith in culture as the one thing that can and must be believed in. For Rieff alienation is symptomatic of a difficult period of transition in contemporary culture. He postulates the emergence of a new cultural type, "psychological man," who is arising from the shambles created by the demise of the old organizing myths of culture. This cultural type aspires "to live with no higher purpose than that of a durable sense of well being" (6:40). The emergent cultural ideal is, then, an unbeliever who views all moral doctrine as absurd. Psychological man is the ultimate pragmatist. Unbound by such absolute visions as finding a "meaningful" life or "doing good," he lives instead an "experimental life" (6:26). He builds his life, and a sense of internal coherence, by utilizing the bits and pieces offered by a fragmented culture. Combining cultivated self-awareness with shrewd insight into his environment, psychological man "is the sane self in a mad world" (6:40). The strategy of living that psychological man embodies would require each individual to sustain a sense of community, a commitment to investing himself in the continuity of culture. It is only by committing themselves to collective beliefs that people can stave off "the infinite variety of panic and emptiness to which they are disposed. It is to control their dis-ease as individuals that men have always acted culturally, in good faith . . . for the control of panic and the filling up of emptiness" (6:3–4).

But it is precisely the traditional belief that acting culturally is in good faith which the experience of alienation directly challenges. The alienated continually declare that people, in acting culturally, act in bad faith. The commitment to culture, they allege, does not control panic or cure the feeling of inner deadness. It results in panicky feelings of emptiness. Commitment to any cultural organizing myth, we are told, is necessarily a form of self-deception. It is thereby tantamount to the negation of self. As Sartre sketches this argument in his discussion of bad faith, the self both denies what it is and constitutes itself in a form of being that it is not. In bad

47

faith one does not merely pretend to be some cultural self, but throws its self into the project of actually becoming the persona in the collective script. This movement toward becoming the not-self is two-sided: it is demanded by society at the same time that it is embraced by the actor as a way of evading himself.

> The waiter in the cafe plays with his condition in order to realize it. This obligation is not different from that which is imposed on all tradesmen. Their condition is wholly one of ceremony. The public demands of them that they realize it as a ceremony; there is the dance of the grocer, of the tailor, of the auctioneer, by which they endeavour to persuade their clientele that they are nothing but a grocer, an auctioneer, a tailor. A grocer who dreams is offensive to the buyer, because such a grocer is not wholly a grocer. Society demands that he limit himself to his function as a grocer, just as the soldier at attention makes himself into a soldier-thing with a direct regard which does not see at all, which is no longer meant to see, since it is the rule and not the interest of the moment which determines the point he must fix his eyes on (the sight "fixed at ten paces"). There are indeed many precautions to imprison a man in what he is, as if we lived in perpetual fear that he might escape from it, that he might break away and suddenly elude his condition (7:11).

The self, for its part, can come to believe that this "dance" is an expression of its own being, rather than a reality to which it must struggle to adhere.

Any attempt to build a culture—sacred or secular—would be a flight away from self and away from release. Secular man is thus not free from fantasy and illusion. His illusion is the belief in culture and that which it can offer him. His faith is that culture will offer him a self that will feel strong and fulfilled. He finds, on the contrary, that this cultural self is a persona or imago. It is all front, all external. The cultural

48

self, devoid of feeling and intention, responds instead to the demands of the social world. Secular man experiences a profound terror at the possibility of violating these demands. The other side of modern man's faith in culture is his dread. He fears that, expelled from culture and its hated bounties, the self would cease to exist. The conflicting perception continues that the demands of culture are mythic, themselves projections and distortions. Defining the self through culture becomes a means of escaping agency and choice. This act of giving up the experience and definition of one's self also provides a rationale for feeling imprisoned.

If we look at the lives men build in our culture and hear them testify to their experiences, the profoundly alienated analyses appear to be more accurate than the hopeful ones. Rieff's unbelievers, he tells us, are in pursuit of pleasure. The formula for this pursuit is to seek, "more of everything—more goods, more housing, more leisure; in short, more life" (6:243). The hunger for more seems, however, insatiable. Slater's observations capture much of the flavor of this eternal questing.

> [O]ne is struck . . . by the grim monotony of American facial expressions—hard, surly, and bitter—and by the aura of deprivation that informs them . . . nothing is done to prepare the returning traveler for the fanatical acquisitiveness of his compatriots. It is difficult to become reaccustomed to seeing people already weighted down with possessions acting as if every object they did not own were bread withheld from a hungry mouth.
>
> These perceptions are heightened by the contrast between the sullen faces of real people and the vision of happiness television offers: men and women ecstatically engaged in stereotyped symbols of fun—running through fields, strolling on beaches, dancing and singing. Smiling faces with chronically open mouths express their gratification with the manifold bounties offered by the culture. One begins to feel

there is a severe gap between the fantasies Americans live by and the realities they live in. Americans know from an early age how they are supposed to look when happy and what they are supposed to do or buy to be happy. But for some reason their fantasies are unrealizable and leave them disappointed and embittered. (7:XII–XIII)

The pursuit of gratifying experience does not represent a means of asserting the self standing outside the culture, or even a means of "using" culture's products. "Pleasure" comes to be no more than another hollow behavioral mode defined by culture. Gratification is linked to the marketplace, to status privileges, and to social characteristics (age, appearance), so that even freedom or fun is something to be obtained from the social system. Feeling or internal experience does not determine self-expression. Expressive behaviors are programmed enactments of a few unimaginative scripts. Indeed, the prepackaged, preformulated quality of fun and pleasure can make them as alienating as regimented work. The key characteristic of both such fun and such work is that they do not come from the self. They exist "out there," and the self merely melds into them.

We therefore do not actually see men who have abandoned culture as a way of organizing self and organizing existence. At most we see people experiencing glimmerings of consciousness about the relations of self to the persona it adopts. This awareness precipitates the emergence of a conflict about the results of acting out any imago that culture can provide. More typically, the self strives to stay within the confines of its persona and to regard the inner despair of existence as caused by external factors. The self turns back to culture to reinforce these strategems.

When looking at data about everyday life, we find, in fact, that the self often seeks to merge with the imago it enacts. The waiter's enactment—like that of the judge or the doctor —can come to be regarded as genuine. The maintenance of this belief depends on collusion between actor and audience. Goffman, a sociologist, is a most astute chronicler of our ritual enactments. He observes that "individuals often foster the impression that the routine they are presently performing is their only routine or at least their most essential one . . . [T]he audience, in their turn, often assumes that the character projected before them is all there is to the individual" (3:48). This reciprocity is highly delicate, requiring mutual cueing between actor and audience, as well as tact, whereby a small divergence from the ideal is overlooked.

In fostering a given impression, Goffman maintains, the actor is exerting a "moral demand" on both himself and the audience. That is, others are obliged "to treat him in the manner that persons of his kind have a right to expect" (3:13). The actor is obliged to stay in role, to forego those behaviors which do not fit the chosen persona. This can often become a struggle, as when one wishes to yawn, stretch, or loosen his clothing. The more respectable the role, the less the actor can indulge in spontaneity.

In time, control of the performance can become very limited. The performer may come to stand on the moral claims he has put forth (for example, to his goodness, his wisdom, or his dedication) and come to need them in order to live with himself. He can "be taken in by his own act . . . [H]e comes to be performer and observer of the same show [concealing from himself any] discreditable facts . . . This intricate maneuver of self delusion constantly occurs" (3:80–81). In this sense the self becomes the illusion it is fostering. As in Sartre's example, "there is no doubt that I am in a sense a cafe waiter—otherwise could I not just as well call myself a diplomat or a reporter? But if I am one, this cannot be in the mode of being in itself. I am a waiter in the mode *of being what I am not*" (7:15).

Sartre's evaluation is not merely a moral judgment. It can only be appreciated in reference to the experience of the actor. Goffman conveniently provides us with information on the experience of self in this mode of being (bad faith). The performer is forced to maintain a kind of eternal vigilance, as if a counter reality were constantly threatening to overwhelm his act. This feeling is most clearly manifest when a performance is, in fact, punctured. It is then that the audience sees a dropping of masks and discovers that "each performer tends to wear a single look, a naked unsocialized look, a look of concentration, a look of one who is privately engaged in a difficult, treacherous task" (3:235). At first glance this would appear to betray anxiety over one's ability to maintain his front. Social participation is partially experienced as a struggle to maintain the moral pose through which one is "recognized." This requires both cooperation with others to foster certain joint realities (Goffman refers to "teamwork"), and an adversary relationship with the rest of the world. Others are waiting to strip the self of its persona should it become lax or overstep its bounds by asking for excessive deference. We can say, then, that one element of existence in bad faith is the continual fear of being revealed. The actor may have no clear notion of a "real self" outside of the image he fosters, but he does know that image to be fraudulent.

Since all actors are vulnerable on this level, Goffman argues, they tend to work at keeping ongoing performances intact. If the performance fails, all masks can lose their validity. At the same time, actors seemingly feel compelled to endanger the performance and the credibility of their own personas. It is observed that:

> [P]erformers rarely seem content with safe channels for expressing discontent with the working consensus. They often attempt to speak out of character in a way that will be heard by the audience but will not openly threaten either the integrity of the two teams or the social distance between them. These temporary unofficial, or controlled, realignments, often aggressive in character, provide an interesting

area for study . . . we may usually detect an unofficial line of communication which each team directs at the other. This unofficial communication may be carried on by innuendo, mimicked accents, well-placed jokes, significant pauses, veiled hints, purposeful kidding, expressive overtone, and many other sign practices. Rules regarding this laxity are quite strict. The communicator has the right to deny that he "meant anything" by his action, should his recipients accuse him to his face of having conveyed something unacceptable, and the recipients have the right to act as if nothing, or only something innocuous, has been conveyed. (3:190–91)

The participants flirt with the possibility of blowing their own covers. The aggressive quality of interchange at the borders of performance seems to be indicative of hostility both to the other and to the self. Goffman provides a most appropriate example in citing from Kincaid's discussion of social life in British-ruled India. The natives would lavishly entertain the occupying colonials. After these gatherings, which were painfully uncomfortable on both sides, there

followed an entertainment of which few British guests were aware. The doors would be shut, and the dancing girls, excellent mimics like all Indians, would give an imitation of the bored guests who had just left, and the uncomfortable tension of the last hour would be dispelled in bursts of happy laughter. And while the English phaetons clattered home Raji and Kaliani would be dressed up to caricature English costume and be executing with indecent exaggeration an Orientalized version of English dances, those minuets and country dances which seemed so innocent and natural to English eyes, so different from the provocative posturing of Indian nautch-girls, but which to Indians appeared utterly scandalous. (3:171–72)

The Indians regarded their guests as fools and buffoons and as profane. Their mockery of the British must, however, be seen as two-edged. They have just humbled themselves before their guests, and know that they will do so again. In going through the enactment of genial host, they have profaned their own homes and their own selves. Hatred of self and of the other go hand in hand. We have many counterparts to this enactment: Goffman mentions the relation of blacks to their "ofay" audience, Jews to the *goyim*, sales people to their customers, and married couples to their guests.

We need not merely infer this double disdain toward self and other which is part of bad faith. Actors, stepping out of role, testify to these feelings. A college student remarks on her behavior in the dating arena:

> I sometimes "play dumb" on dates, but it leaves a bad taste. The emotions are complicated. Part of me enjoys "putting something over" on the unsuspecting male. But this sense of superiority over him is mixed with feelings of guilt for my hypocrisy. Toward the "date" I feel some contempt because he is "taken in" by my technique, or if I like the boy, a kind of maternal condescension . . .

> And the funny part of it is that the man, I think, is not always so unsuspecting. He may sense the truth and become uneasy in the relation. "Where do I stand? Is she laughing up her sleeve or did she mean this praise? . . . And once or twice I felt that the joke was on me; the boy saw through my wiles and felt contempt for me for stooping to such tricks. (3:236–37)

There are, then, a number of emotional counterparts to role behavior; they involve fear and anxiety over being turned out of one's role, of being exposed as a "fraud." This fear is, at the same time, ambivalent. The tension of sustaining the persona is stressful. The counterwish to step out of role continues to press for expression. The experience of being corrupted by one's own duplicity leads to a yearning for "natural" expression. It would seem, however, that actors do not simply express their longing and abandon their roles. Instead, they look for little releases, little pockets of privacy where they can be themselves. Wishing to be themselves, they are bewildered over what action to take. The closest they can come to expressing something real is in being negative about their own continual fraudulence. This rather limited self-liberation takes the form of satirizing and complaining about their usual role enactments. But griping leads to no positive self-assertions. Actors can conceive of no action that will make them feel much better, but they experience circumstances as the basis for this problem. The self keeps claiming—without any apparent evidence—that it would transcend its misery if only reality were not so oppressive. Negative attribution tends always to be directed outward. It is the "other" (as audience or co-performer) who is unworthy, troublesome, and counterfeit.

Because the "middle Americans" express these perceptions with remarkable clarity, they can increase our understanding of what it is like to live in this state of conflict and yearning. They are aware, for example, of enacting the dance of the shopkeeper. A wife describes her husband, the owner of a drugstore. He is, she tells us, "just a druggist" (2:173). It is unclear whether she means that he is no more than this role, or the role is less than significant, or both. When at the store,

> Paul has to keep smiling all day long. It really makes a difference to the customers. He says that when he's feeling bad, with a cold or something, his business goes down that day. It just does. I used to think he was exaggerating. But I've been in the store, and I've seen how he really sells, oh does he, when he's in a good frame of mind and all smiles. He goes after the customers, and he tries to help them, and he reminds them of what they may want to buy, and he asks questions—whether they forgot this or that. He's not pushy. That's no good. He's the gentleman that he is, that's

what; and then they go and buy a few extra things, and of course it helps them, because they don't have to make so many trips. (2:176)

This behavior constitutes most of Paul's waking life. He works long hours for six days of the week and also opens his store on Sunday mornings. The wife recognizes that on Sunday "Paul has to open for those few hours. It spoils the day, but he can't help it. A lot of business comes in" (2:176). The necessity for behaving as one does, no matter how abhorrent it may seem, is a common theme in this woman's conception of reality. She quotes a neighbor, "who keeps on saying that no one has much choice anymore; that unless you have money . . . then you're just going to be pushed around and pushed around" (2:127). One's own behavior is thus experienced as having little to do with intention. It is, rather, dictated by the demands of "reality." Paul neatly disowns his own behavior at work by dissociating himself from his cronies at the Junior Chamber of Commerce. "He doesn't feel he's a Chamber of Commerce type. A lot of them, they're too ambitious" (2: 176).

Although Paul and his wife are able to block out some of the characteristics of his behavior, their denial is only partially successful. The wife knows that he is a "tough, able, shrewd businessman" (2:179). We have here at least two levels of deception or sham. First, the smiling helpful shopkeeper is the illusion of self fostered to deal with the world. Paul, as we have heard, is self-consciously aware that the function of this persona is to increase revenues. He keeps his aggressiveness in bounds, and begins to believe that his selling really "helps them." Indeed, this is the other half of the wife's image of Paul. She regards him as "so soft, so generous, so concerned with people that 'it's a wonder he charges them anything at all' " (2:179). We cannot say that Paul totally accepts the illusion he attempts to foster, but he works hard at believing in it.

Feelings of unreality about self seem to creep in the back

door and stay poorly defined. This couple exhibits a sense of disbelief about where they are in life. They express the feeling that perhaps they don't deserve to be there. They indicate that ownership of the store was stumbled into by "mere luck" (2: 173). In the few quiet moments they have, the two seem to be shaking their heads in disbelief. "We feel that we're more fortunate than we could ever have expected . . . Sometimes . . . Paul is getting dressed and so am I, and he'll look at me and say he can't figure out how we did it, but we did. And I'll agree" (2:174).

The feeling of unreality, of an insubstantial quality to their existence, is also reflected in a vague sense of impending disaster. Paul, we are told "gets nervous sometimes. He gets afraid we won't ever pay off the drug store, so it's really ours" (2: 175). The image that haunts them is of the Depression, although both are much too young to have experienced it. The wife speaks of her father's dreams being dashed when his farm failed in 1938. Paul, in fact, "talks a lot about it, the economy" (2:175). They don't really understand the economy, they admit, but Paul senses that his own well being is linked to it. Another depression seems unlikely, "but who knows—not us" (2:175).

These two give the sense that they are confused and frightened. They feel out of place, moving in and out of immersion in the imagos they strive to become. Occasionally, glimpses of the hunger beneath show through: "Once she said she wanted so many things she had to stop herself from thinking about them all, because there is a limit, an absolute limit, to the greed a person ought to let himself reveal, even to himself" (2:179). Their apprehensiveness and sense of deprivation seem to be common elements in the presentations Coles records. The author finds a nonreligious "sense of foreboding . . . based on the conviction that God's prescriptions (or merely the normal or tried and true or familiar customs) are somehow endangered" (2:142).

The danger usually is seen emanating from the "other." His

guises are "long hair," "hippie," "the colored" and "the affluent types." These deviants are loud, overly critical, reformist,
self-centered, morally lax, and sexually wanton. They are
troublemakers, too greedy and grabby: they want something
for nothing. Welfare is particularly enraging to the middle
Americans, especially as they believe it is abused by the
blacks: "They loaf around, and the taxpayer has to support
them, while the rest of us work . . . And their husbands sneak
in and out, so the women are eligible for welfare. It's a dis-
grace!" (2:100).

There is a personal kind of rage felt toward those who are
"ruining our country." The middle American feels himself being robbed, abused, taken advantage of at every turn.

There is a working alliance (conspiracy?) of people above
and below them in the social structure. The blacks "are getting
away with something [because] they have the support of rich
and powerful people" (2:100). If the Blacks are seen as lazy
and willing to take all they can "con the rest of us into giving
them," the real culprits are the well to do. "Rich liberals" and
corporations (2:105) are making life intolerable for ordinary
people. The middle Americans are victimized, they tell us, by
these entrenched power elites. A father grieves the recent loss
of a son in Vietnam:

> I'm bitter. You bet your goddam dollar I'm bitter. It's peo-
> ple like us who give up our sons for the country. The busi-
> ness people, they run the country and make money from it.
> The college types, the professors, they go to Washington
> and tell the government what to do. Do this, they say; do
> that. But their sons, they don't end up in the swamps over
> there, in Vietnam. No sir. They're deferred, because they're
> in school. Or they get sent to safe places. Or they get out
> with all those letters they have from their doctors. (2:131)

This man does not perceive himself as having sacrificed in a
worthy cause. He has been robbed of his most beloved possession by those with wealth, status, and influence. Moreover, he

experiences this loss as but a symptom of his general status as victim. Others have visibility, power, and abundance. The self is but one of the deprived mass. One's goodness and adherence to duty are never rewarded. Fair play only handicaps the self, making one more vulnerable to the less scrupulous.

Another man works as a loan officer in a bank and moonlights as an armed guard in a warehouse owned by the bank president. He seems to feel debased and powerless, working for despised interests. He describes his father waking in the night to "shout and scream at the rich people, 'selfish' he'd call them . . . selfish, selfish, selfish. Sometimes I'll be busy at work . . . but suddenly I'll hear him saying 'selfish' " (2:93). These same rich people, as he knows from his contact with the bank trustees, can call upon their congressman for favors. They control the news media and can push their views in a way that the ordinary man never could.

The middle American experiences himself as powerless to change his existence, or even to defend himself. "The world doesn't hear me," he says, "and it doesn't hear a single person I know" (2:134). The world becomes a largely terrifying, alien place to him: "I hate going into town. I'm afraid all the way that I'll be robbed and beaten . . . The police don't really protect you. They try to but their hands are tied" (2:104). The same hated alliance of the underclass and the rich liberals has created this plight. The affluent keep calling for understanding and fair play for criminals, but "Who feels sorry for the people those criminals attack?" (2:104).

This last remark is representative of a whole class of feelings which emerge around the issue of victimization. These people keep communicating a kind of neediness, a very basic sense of deprivation that they are reluctant to admit. They feel deprived of love, recognition, selfhood. Coles writes of the family that has lost a son in the war. These "two American parents, owners of a home that has in it a refrigerator, a washing machine, a toaster, a waffle iron, a television set and a car, feel poor, feel lost, feel confused, feel cheated" (2:130).

The father recalls a dream that may express the depths of their hunger:

> I was in the supermarket and I put all the stuff on the counter, and the girl added it up and I didn't have enough money to pay. Then she told me to put everything back on the shelves, and I said no, I couldn't because we'd all starve to death. Then Ralph came into the store and he said if he could get killed like he did, then the store could forget about the extra couple of dollars—and they did, I think. The last thing I remember, I was still arguing with them, the manager and the checker, but they were nodding at me while I gave it to them. I must have been shouting. That's when my wife woke me up. (2:133)

If this hunger is metaphoric, what does it symbolize? The things being withheld are necessities: without them one would starve. The protagonist has the right to them because of his goodness, because he has sacrificed for the group. Ralph, the son, has been transformed by death into a moral claim. The claim, however, is made not in strength but in a passive, pleading voice. It is not as ironclad as having "enough money to pay." This man "always says that what matters in this world is that you can pay your bills. Then you can look any man alive in the face, and not be ashamed" (2:133). To lack money is to be weak, a beggar. Ralph's father keeps striving to maintain this image of manhood, yet the very endeavor makes him feel deprived and exploited. We hear evidence that even as he vigorously disowns these feelings, he yearns for sympathy and concern. "He shouts sometimes that the peace people are so busy feeling sorry for Hanoi and for their people, and for the colored we have here at home, that they don't stop and think about us, all of us who have given our sons, lost our sons to the enemy" (2:133). This man hates the antiwar forces because of their insincerity, because they don't care for him enough. Suspecting that his son died for no good reason, he refuses to accept the idea of surrender in the war.

The middle American, it must be recognized, continually works to maintain a scenario in which he feels oppressed and misused. Our bank officer, who so passionately condemns the monied interests, tells us: "When I'm in the bank I'm more likely to be tough on our customers. I'm out to do the best I can for the bank" (2:91). This man is not totally without perspective. He sees the madness he is immersed in, the madness he is helping to perpetuate. The image of society he reveals to Coles is that "everybody wants what he can get, and then he wants more, and he's never satisfied, and that's what keeps the country going . . . people thinking they have to *have* things, and coming to us for the money, and then sweating themselves into an early grave paying us back" (2:92).

If this man perceives some of the nightmarish quality of his own existence (and that of the people around him), he feels generally powerless and blameless in relation to it. The entrenched elites who control the country are responsible: he is but their helpless tool and victim. The man perceives himself as one of the mass that is being ripped off. He expresses, for example, suspicion why interest rates are so high (2:92) the same time he condemns the "unpatriotic," the "noisy college students always trying to get out of their responsibilities" (2:93). He feels repressive hatred for those who would overturn the system he claims to abhor. He can recognize the absurdity of such a position in others, but not in himself.

An elderly woman comes in to request a loan. She launches into a tirade, accusing bankers of keeping interest rates artificially high to increase their profits. The loan officer reports incredulously:

> that old lady, she went on and on about "the few" who are ruining America, and making it tough on the rest of us. Then, you know what she told me? She's a member of the John Birch Society, and so is her son and her two daughters and their husbands! I couldn't help myself. I said, "Lady, how will the John Birch Society change things in this

country?" She said that when the conspiracy is exposed, that's ruining the country, we'd be better off. The way she sees it, the big bankers and people like that have been taken in by the Communists, and they're all set upon ruining the country, and making more money while they do, and then the Russians will take over. Now, she's just crazier than the others, but you ought to hear people talk! (2:92)

Evil becomes twice removed. Not only is one being manipulated by invisible others, but the others are in turn being duped and used by distant powers. The middle American transforms his anger so that the enemy is he who opposes the guiding ideals of the system.

We can add another ingredient to these mixed perceptions. The middle American expresses a certain longing to be like those who embody evil: the protesters and the "big shots." A machinist tells Coles: "I'll admit I have my complaints. Sometimes I think I'd like to start protesting myself." On the same occasion he admits that "there will be some days I'll regret I'm not a lawyer, or some big shot" (2:43). One might assume that this man is an "enlightened" blue collar worker, unlike the other people under discussion. His comments toward the end of the same interview dispel this notion. "I hate cities . . . to me cities are where city slickers live, businessmen and lawyers and that type, and the colored people, who wants any part of them? Not me, I'll tell you that" (2:43).

The "middle Americans" may be more than a segment of our culture. They may, in many ways, embody it. Their feelings, concerns, fantasies, and ideology revolve around a common, finite scenario. Its constituent elements are misery, greed, and longing. We hear over and over a sense of deprivation and the feeling that one is acting as a servile will, the instrument of unseen and unreachable forces. One is surrounded by these hostile forces, all having illegitimate power over the self. The middle American, in his own conception of himself, embodies rectitude. He is decent and moral. He deserves more, but it is being withheld from him because of his very goodness. His deprivation is seen as the result of his refusal to steal, protest, and beg: these are the weapons of the "others." The middle American feels uninvolved in the creation of his own fate and powerless to alter the oppressiveness of his existence.

These people do not seem to experience an absence of community, nor do they exhibit secular skepticism. Community or culture is seen as a substantial, oppressive force in their lives. They report themselves as being burdened and trapped by the weight of community, and yearn to be free of it.

Sensing some of his own feelings of rage, the middle American backs away from them and disowns them. He recognizes many of the absurd features of the universe he has constructed, but feels paralyzed in the face of them. He exhibits the need both to articulate his misery and remain immersed in it. Very occasionally, the sense of his own agency in creating and maintaining his existence is expressed. The bank officer again talks of his father: "He'd start blaming the people for putting up with what they do . . . 'People get what they deserve' . . . He'd say that if people wanted a better country, they'd have one" (2:93).

These elements add up to feelings of disdain toward the self, and envy, fear, and hatred toward others. They are often associated with an impotent wish which, as we have heard, takes two forms. On the one hand, the middle American hopes for a transformation of culture, a redressing of the balance. This is the means by which he will be relieved of the short end of the stick and get that which he "deserves" and covets. We also know that he works to negate this possibility, to fight against change as indecent and cataclysmic. The second form of the wish he harbors is escape, leaving culture to stand alone as himself. It is this metaphor of escape which is shared by the middle American and the culture of discontent. It may be expressive of the feelings that are common to many varieties of alienation.

References

1. Bruno Bettelheim, Statement before House Special Subcommittee on Education. March 20, 1969, recounted in *U.S. News and World Report* (April 7, 1969), pp. 47–48.
2. Robert Coles, *The Middle Americans*, Boston, Little Brown (1971).
3. Erving Goffman, *The Presentation of Self in Everyday Life*, Garden City, New York, Doubleday Anchor (1959).
4. Kenneth Kenniston, *The Uncommitted*, New York, Delta Books (1965).
5. Z. J. Lipowski, "The Conflict of Buridan's Ass or Some Dilemmas of Affluence: The Theory of Attractive Stimulus Overload," *American Journal of Psychiatry*, 127:273–279 (1970).
6. Philip Rieff, *The Triumph of the Therapeutic*, New York, Harper and Row (1966).
7. Jean-Paul Sartre, *Existential Psychoanalysis*, Chicago, Regency (1962), pp. 182–183.
8. P. Slater, *The Pursuit of Loneliness*, Boston, Beacon Press (1970).
9. A. Toffler, *Future Shock*, New York, Random House (1970).

3. The Journey into Silence

At the end of *Catch-22* Yossarian decides to desert from the Air Force and flee to Sweden. He can no longer tolerate the collective madness and murderousness of which he is a part. The act is a consequence of his awakening, an assertion of life. He announces his decision, and someone asks, " 'How do you feel, Yossarian?' 'Fine. No, I'm very frightened.' 'That's good,' said Major Danby, 'It proves you're still alive. It won't be fun.' 'Yes it will' " (3:463). Thus commences Yossarian's flight; a flight away from the absurd. Heller leaves us hanging. He doesn't state the nature of the challenge facing the self as it attempts to stand outside of culture. Indeed, Yossarian— like all the alienated—feels he must flee regardless of what results aloneness might bring. Escape is both exhilarating and terrifying.

Bellow's *Herzog* and Ellison's *Invisible Man* represent two attempts to explore the nature of this journey. In explicating the agony of their protagonists, both authors attempt to give form to the anguish that underlies the sense of alienation. They present visions of men struggling to give up belief in history. Herzog and Invisible Man, in striving to disengage from a culture they regard as a living death, find that they must confront themselves. Their battle evolves away from a heroic struggle against other men who are oppressing them. The core of their mission becomes a confrontation with the inner turmoil that leads them to act in bad faith by engaging culture rather than trying to live with themselves. They discover, that is, their own complicity in creating the nightmare fantasy that causes their suffering. Moving out of the fantasy requires them to accept this truth, requires the willingness to live with themselves as their own oppressors.

We first encounter Herzog in a frenzy of communication: "He had fallen under a spell and was writing letters to everyone under the sun" (1:1). In writing them he is seeking something from the world. He is trying to end his own agony and confusion by having others endorse him, offer sympathy and affirm his goodness. He feels "the need to explain, to have it out, to justify, to put into perspective, to clarify, to make amends" (1:2).

Herzog is engaged in what appears to be two separate battles with reality, the one mundane, the other glorious. He is desperate to right the wrong that has been done him by his second wife, Madeleine, and his former best friend. The two had used him, carried on an adulterous affair, and finally tossed him out. Herzog is also suffering from the separation from his young daughter, and his fear that she is being abused by the two lovers. In this particular subdrama the protagonist feels himself to be both victim and gallant saviour. He believes, in retrospect, that everyone (in-laws, friends, attorney) had been plotting against him. They had, he sees, all known about the affair and kept him in the dark while helping the lovers to meet. They were conspiring to rob him of both money and daughter through the divorce settlement. To heal the wounds inflicted by this experience, to relieve the anger and self-hatred he feels, Herzog yearns for vengeance against Madeleine and Gersbach.

On a second level Herzog is trying to wrestle reality into some kind of order or comprehensibility. His ambition is to rectify the problem of pointlessness: "people can be free now but the freedom doesn't have any content. It's like a howling emptiness" (1:39). Herzog's formula for escaping the dilemma is in a book he is writing, but the enterprise is an endless spinning of wheels. The notes for the book lay in a closet, "eight hundred pages of chaotic argument which never found its focus" (1:4). He feels impelled to impose some overriding truth on the world in order to harness the chaos that plagues him. One of his letters is a rambling dissertation to a former tutor. Toward the end he writes:

> "Annihilation is no longer a metaphor. Good and Evil are real. The inspired condition is therefore no visionary matter. It is not reserved for gods, kings, poets, priests, shrines, but belongs to mankind and to all of existence. And therefore—"
>
> Therefore, Herzog's thought, like those machines in the lofts he had heard yesterday in the taxi, stopped by traffic in the garment district, plunged and thundered with endless —infinite—hungry, electrical power, stitching fabric with inexhaustible energy. Having seated himself again in his striped jacket he was gripping the legs of his desk between his knees, his teeth set, the straw hat cutting his forehead. He wrote, "Reason exists! Reason . . ." he then heard the soft dense rumbling of falling masonry, the splintering of wood and glass. "And belief based on reason. Without which the disorder of the world will never be controlled by mere organization." (1:165)

Herzog attempts to penetrate, at the most abstract level, the mysteries of being and meaning. His quest is juxtaposed to the fact that, in regard to his own life, he has been a fool. As the plaster ceiling of his crumbling mansion falls on his head, Herzog propounds the power of reason and order. He visits Madeleine's aunt Zelda. She points out that his marital troubles started when he moved to Ludeyville, a remote Berkshire town, to write his book. Zelda also points out that the book was never finished, and questions the point of the whole venture.

Herzog tried to explain what it was about—that his study

was supposed to have ended with a new angle on the modern condition, showing how life could be lived by renewing universal connections; overturning the last of the Romantic errors about the uniqueness of the Self; revising the old Western, Faustian ideology; investigating the social meaning of Nothingness. And more. But he checked himself, for she did not understand, and this offended her, especially as she believed she was no common hausfrau. She said, "It sounds very grand. Of course it must be important. But that's not the point. You were a fool to bury yourself and her, a young woman, in the Berkshires, with nobody to talk to."

"Except Valentine Gersbach . . ." (1:39)

Herzog flees from the inability to deal with the immediacy of his life to the realm of philosophical abstraction. In both realms he pursues the "answer," the golden key that will give him a sense of meaning. This answer, Herzog assumes, is to be found in culture. His life's work is rummaging through the materials of high culture—Romanticism, Christianity, Faustian ideology—to find the new arrangement that will make mankind feel at peace with itself. The quest for answers is, of course, a frantic flight from immediacy. Herzog cannot bear to recognize what he is and what he does to himself and others. In his personal agony he runs from acquaintance to relative to friend in the hope of finding comfort. His self is, as he phrases it, "a collective project." He has given up the experience of control over his actions:

he had been taking this primitive cure, administered by Madeleine, Sandor, et cetera; so that his recent misfortunes might be seen as a collective project, himself participating, to destroy his vanity and his pretensions to a personal life so that he might disintegrate and suffer and hate, like so many others, not on anything so distinguished as a cross, but down in the mire or post-Renaissance, post-humanistic, post-Cartesian dissolution, next door to the Void. (1:93)

In serving himself up to others, Herzog has spread himself across reality, and encounters himself in symbolic form wherever he looks. Feeling himself the victim of reality, he draws no boundaries between himself and those he identifies as fellow sufferers. He writes a letter to Dr. Bhave, a spiritual leader in India:

> "Recently, I saw Pather Panchali. I assume you know it, since the subject is rural India. Two things affected me greatly—the old crone scooping the mush with her fingers and later going into the weeds to die; and the death of the young girl in the rains." Herzog, almost alone in the Fifth Avenue Playhouse, cried with the child's mother when the hysterical death music started. Some musician with a native brass horn, imitating sobs, playing a death noise. It was raining also in New York, as in rural India. His heart was aching. He too had a daughter, and his mother too had been a poor woman. He had slept on sheets made of flour sacks. The best type for the purpose was Ceresota. (1:48)

As Herzog recounts his history and his troubles, we realize that he has consistently chosen to move into this oppressed position. He had abandoned both his beautiful first wife and his lovely and willing mistress in his passion for Madeleine. Herzog had many warnings of her castrating, capricious style, but simply could not tolerate peace or gratification. He felt compelled to give up "the shelter of an orderly, purposeful, lawful existence because it bored me" (1:103). Herzog instead leaps at the opportunity to abandon himself to Madeleine. Everyone around him can see the self-destruction this entails. At Madeleine's request Herzog visits her father to seek approval for their union. The older man inquires " 'In love with my daughter?' 'Yes.' 'It isn't doing much for your health, I see.' 'I haven't been too well, Mr. Pontritter' " (1:107).

Herzog finds in Madeleine a heroic struggle, a way to degrade himself and make himself miserable while feeling virtuous. Tennie, Madeleine's mother, has a long talk with him about her daughter. Tennie "manipulates" him, Herzog tells us, but he is aware of what's going on. Herzog is simply being "carried away" by the metaphor of what he thinks he is doing. "He listened to Tennie very thoughtfully—for a man whose mind had stopped working. It was too full of grand projects to think of anything very clearly" (1:109). Tennie convinces him, and Herzog convinces himself, that Madeleine is but a "headstrong, deluded child" (1:109) and that his "patience, loving kindness, and virility" will straighten her out. Herzog tries to become the knight in shining armor. Madeleine is simultaneously the fire-breathing dragon and the damsel in distress. In conquering and possessing her, Herzog hopes to feel alive.

Herzog's marriage to Madeleine instead plunges him into misery and a sense of servitude. "There was a flavor of subjugation in his love for Madeleine. Since she was domineering, and since he loved her, he had to accept the flavor that was given" (1:8). Herzog never tries actively to conquer Madeleine, but instead attempts to mollify her. He entertains their child as Madeleine trysts with her paramour. Herzog subsequently enacts the scenario of the wounded lover with quasi-aware-ness but also with resignation or helplessness. He partially senses its unreality but is nonetheless affected by it. In a final showdown Madeleine tells him that she no longer loves him and he must leave. Herzog thinks to himself: "Her sentences were well formed. This speech had been rehearsed and it also seemed that he had been waiting for the performance to be-gin" (1:9). If Madeleine is staging a dramatic and cruel scenario, Herzog plays his parts as straight man (wounded party) and audience with perfect decorum. His sense of expec-tation can only mean that he has known all along what he has been getting himself into.

Herzog even has some fleeting sense of his purpose in making an absurd mess of his life. As Madeleine's little speech unfolds, he thinks, "What he was about to suffer, he deserved: he had sinned long and hard; he had earned it. This was it" (1:8).

70

Herzog's purposes are, of course, more complex than a simple desire for punishment. He stage manages a scenario in which he feels made to suffer by the wrongdoing of others. He can then feel wounded, aggrieved—feel that his existence is being dissolved by some force outside of himself. Screaming for reason and humanity, he finds ways to plunge himself into chaos and to provide himself with moral justifications for murder. He is seeking sympathy from everyone, but most of all from himself. At the same time, he feels sickened by his own enterprise. "He noted with distaste his own trick of appealing for sympathy. A personality had its own ways. A mind might observe without approval. Herzog did not care for his own personality, and at the moment there was apparently nothing he could do about its impulses" (1:12).

Herzog feels carried away by the drama of his life. His own part, like that of his counterplayers, seems to be determined by mysterious impulses emanating from something that is not himself. He is even a helpless observer of the doings of his own personality. Feeling trapped, he experiences his existence as unreal. He senses something shabby and vague about his heartache and moral suffering. "Moses hated the humiliating comedy of heartache. But can thought wake you from the dream of existence? Not if it becomes a second realm of confusion, another more complicated dream, the dream of intellect, the delusion of total explanations" (1:166).

This is precisely the way in which Herzog attempts to use intellect and philosophy. In divorcing thought from the reality of his experience, he renders his intellectual passion impotent: it can neither add to the synthesis of ideas he seeks, nor change his life. His struggle is a complicated attempt to experience a proposition he can glibly write but not apply to his own being: "people can be free now" (1:39). To experience this freedom he must strip himself of illusion, pretense, bad faith. This is a two-pronged movement: his romantic idealism crumbles as his desire to avenge himself on Madeleine and Gersbach dissolves. He begins to sense the cleavage between his philosophical abstractions and the agony of his being.

He calls Simkin, his lawyer. In doing so he is uncertain of his own purposes, except that he is concerned about the welfare of his daughter, who is living with Madeleine and Gersbach in Chicago. He has heard indirectly that the girl had been left sitting alone in a car on the streets of Chicago. The news has filled him with rage, and with the impulse to save her from abuse and neglect by his ex-wife and his ex-friend.

Herzog confesses to Simkin that he cannot grasp Gersbach's essential secret—his essence:

"Do you mean to say that all those philosophers you've studied for so many years are all frustrated by one Valentine Gersbach?" said Simkin. "All those years of Spinoza—Hegel?"

"You're ribbing me, Simkin."

"Sorry. That wasn't a good joke."

"I don't mind. It seems true. Like taking swimming lessons on the kitchen table. Well, I can't answer for the philosophers. Maybe power philosophy, Thomas Hobbes, could analyze him. But when I think of Valentine I don't think of philosophy, I think of the books I devoured as a boy, on the French and Russian revolutions. And silent movies, like *Mme. Sans Gene*—Gloria Swanson. Or Emil Jannings as a Czarist general. Anyway, I see the mobs breaking into the palaces and churches and sacking Versailles, wallowing in cream deserts or pouring wine over their dicks and dressing in purple velvet, snatching crowns and miters and crosses . . ."

Herzog knew very well when he talked like this that he was again in the grip of that eccentric, dangerous force that had been capturing him. It was at work now, and he felt himself bending. At any moment he might hear a crack. He must stop this. He heard Simkin laughing softly and steadily to himself on his fat chest, and wrinkles of cheerful satire in play about his bushy eyes and hairy ears. "Emancipation

resulting in madness. Unlimited freedom to choose and play
a tremendous variety of roles with a lot of coarse energy."
(1:215–16)

Gersbach fascinates Herzog (produces hate, envy, and rage
in him), because he represents a part of himself that Herzog
cannot get in tune with. Gersbach is vitality, energy, potency
with no purpose other than his own experience. Gersbach is
emancipated, he acts while Herzog can only be obsessive and
ruminate. Gersbach is madness in its most threatening sense.
He treats the world as if it were a void in which he can create
his own reality. Herzog regards himself as one of those "young
Jews brought up on moral principles as Victorian ladies were
on pianoforte and needlepoint" (1:321). He recognizes these
other possibilities, other sectors of his being outside of the
"moral principles," which constrict and blind him. He feels
impelled to confront this reality, just as he had felt impelled
to seek closeness with Gersbach.

Herzog goes to court to find Simken, commenting, "I have
come here today for a look at something different. That evidently is my purpose" (1:321). The defendants, more than
Hegel and Spinoza, help Herzog to see the ways by which he
and other men constitute a world they regard as real. There is
the mad scenario of a German intern who placed his hand on
a vice squad detective's sexual organ in the men's room of
Grand Central Station. There is a boy with dyed hair who
answers to the name "Alice" or "Aleck" depending on what
people want him for. Herzog asks himself:

What view of things was this Aleck advancing? He seemed
to be giving the world comedy for comedy, joke for joke.
With his dyed hair, like the winter-beaten wool of a sheep,
and his round eyes, traces of mascara still on them, the
tight provocative pants, and something sheeplike, too, even
about his vengeful merriment, he was a dream actor. With
his bad fantasy he defied a bad reality, subliminally asserting
to the magistrate, "Your authority and my degeneracy are

73

one and the same." Yes, it must be something like that, Herzog decided. Sandor Himmelstein declared with rage that every living soul was a whore. Of course the magistrate had not spread his legs literally; but he must have done all that was necessary within the power structure to get appointed. Still, nothing about him denied such charges, either. His face was illusionless, without need of hypocrisy. (1:299)

Herzog senses his communality with Aleck and with the intern. All of them are living in a nightmare existence in which one is alternately rapist and victim. As Herzog sees that the boundaries of his life are being determined by his own personal nightmare, he senses that being "in pain. He should be. Quite right. If only because he had required so many people to lie to him, many, many, beginning, naturally, with his mother" (1:232).

At the boundary of the dream, one finds the pain of awakening. Herzog yearns to awaken from his nightmare but is terrified to undo the web of lies which has been his life. He therefore plunges back into his dream and renews his mission of vengeance against Madeleine and Gersbach. He resolves that he must kill them in order to save his daughter. But he cannot do it. "To shoot him!" thinks Herzog as he looks in the bathroom window of Madeleine's house where Gersbach is bathing his daughter, "an absurd thought":

As soon as Herzog saw the actual person giving an actual bath, the reality of it, the tenderness of such a buffoon to a little child, his intended violence turned into *theater*, into something ludicrous. He was not ready to make such a complete fool of himself because his heart was "broken". How could it be broken by such a pair? Lingering in the alley awhile, he congratulated himself on his luck. His breath came back to him; and how good it felt to breathe! It was worth the trip. (1:258)

This inability to murder in the name of righteousness is not part of Herzog's obsessive madness. It is his first movement toward awareness, toward real action in a real world.

Herzog has begun to sense that he has constituted a world of imagos and that all his verbiage has been an attempt to convince himself that these imagos are real. "I go after reality with language," he tells his friend:

> Perhaps I'd like to change it all into language, to force Madeleine and Gersbach to have a *Conscience*. There's a word for you. I must be trying to keep tight the tensions without which human beings can no longer be called human. If they don't suffer, they've gotten away from me. And I've filled the world with letters to prevent their escape. I want them in human form, and so I conjure up a whole environment and catch them in the middle. I put my whole heart into these constructions. But they are constructions. (1:272)

As his personal, vindictive struggle with reality loses its reality, so does the philosophical abstraction that had been the other pillar of his existence. He begins to see how such grand schemes serve as vehicles and justifications for the nightmare. This movement is anticipated earlier in the book, when Herzog is discussing his wife with their analyst. The psychiatrist asks Herzog if Madeleine held a "Christian outlook." He answers in his rambling, professorial style: "I don't agree with Nietzsche that Jesus made the whole world sick, infected it with his slave morality. But Nietzsche himself had a Christian view of history, seeing the present moment always as some crisis, some fall from classical greatness, some corruption or evil to be saved from. I call that Christian. And Madeleine has it, all right. To some extent many of us do. Think we have to recover from some poison, need saving, ransoming. Madeleine wants a savior, and for her I'm no savior." (1:54) Nietzsche has built his view of history on the very assumption that characterizes Madeleine's and Herzog's bad faith. Both live as if they were being victimized by some terrible stroke of fate, some malevolence in the outer world. They, like Nietzsche's superman, must stop at nothing in their attempts to recoup this loss or they shall perish. History and madness are inseparable. Both represent men enacting their bad faith, bringing to life these internal metaphors that account for their suffering while exonerating them from their own acts. Herzog thinks about a book written by an acquaintance.

It was not terribly original, this idea of Shapiro's, but he did a good clear job. *In my review I tried to suggest that clinical psychologists might write fascinating histories. Put professionals out of business. Megalomania for the Pharaohs and Caesars. Melancholia in the Middle Ages. Schizophrenia in the eighteenth century. And then this Bulgarian, Banowitch, seeing all power struggles in terms of paranoid mentality*—a curious, creepy mind, that one, convinced that madness always rules the world. The Dictator must have living crowds and also a crowd of corpses. The vision of mankind as a lot of cannibals, running in packs, gibbering, bewailing its own murders, pressing out the living world as dead excrement. Do not deceive yourself, dear Moses Elkanah, with childish jingles and Mother Goose. Hearts quaking with cheap and feeble charity or oozing potato love have not written history. Shapiro's snarling teeth, his salivating greed, the dagger of an ulcer in his belly give him true insights, too. Fountains of human blood that squirted from fresh graves! Limitless massacre! I never understood it! (1:77)

If the world that men have collectively created is madness, where does one turn to experience reality? To play one's own part in the collective dream, Herzog senses, can lead only to nausea, the sense of living as something unreal. He can therefore turn to no one for help. No one can liberate him from the prison of unreality he shares with other men. He thinks, "I am Herzog. I have *to be* that man. No one else can do it

. . . he must return to his own self and see the thing through"
(1:69).

Herzog's odyssey is a continual, tortuous, reconsideration of
this notion. He must examine it and try to enact it in every
facet of his existence until he finally feels the strength and
desperation to incorporate it, to shuck off the dream. Herzog
gives up his letter writing, his attempt to mold "constructions"
in which he cannot believe. Others regard this withdrawal as
madness, but he senses that it is the only possible pathway to
reality. Herzog resolves to "do no more to enact the peculiarities of life":

> He turned his dark face toward the house again. He went
> around and entered from the front, wondering what further
> evidence of his sanity, besides refusing to go to the hospital,
> he could show. Perhaps he'd stop writing letters. Yes, that
> was what was coming, in fact. The knowledge that he was
> done with these letters. Whatever had come over him during
> these last months, the spell, really seemed to be passing,
> really going. He set down his hat, with the roses and day
> lilies, on the half-painted piano, and went into his study,
> carrying the wine bottles in one hand like a pair of Indian
> clubs. Walking over notes and papers, he lay down on his
> Recamier couch. As he stretched out, he took a long breath,
> and then he lay, looking at the mesh of the screen, pulled
> loose by vines, and listening to the steady scratching of Mrs.
> Tuttle's broom. He wanted to tell her to sprinkle the floor.
> She was raising too much dust. In a few minutes he would
> call down to her. "Damp it down, Mrs. Tuttle. There's
> water in the sink." But not just yet. At this time he had no
> messages for anyone. Nothing. Not a single word. (1:341)

As Herzog ends his journey in aloneness and silence, so does
Invisible Man. Herzog's Ludeyville finds its counterpart in
Invisible Man's walled off section of basement in an all-white
apartment house on the border of Harlem. Both retreats are,

77

as Herzog's brother observes, "*In drerd aufn deck*. The edge of nowhere. Out on the lid of Hell" (1:329). Like Herzog, Invisible Man chooses this domain over what others represent to be the "real world."

The collective world, Invisible Man declares, is no more than "a nightmare which the sleeper tries with all his strength to destroy" (2:7). To destroy the nightmare is to awaken, to know as Herzog knows that "men can be free . . ." Invisible Man's odyssey is a tortuous, ambivalent movement toward his perception. At the same time that he is repelled by the nightmare, he clings to it. To awaken he must give up his belief in finding salvation through history. Like Herzog he begins his quest by assuming that a sense of inner peace and self worth can be found only through history, through the affirmation of other men.

In order to maintain such a belief, he must refuse to accept that which continually confronts him. He must continually deny the oppressive, brutal, fraudulent quality of social reality. This is Invisible Man's "naiveté," the "sickness" for which he must seek a cure. As he declares, he is separated from his own life because he has not achieved the "realization that everyone else appears to have been born with: that I am nobody but myself" (2:19). Lacking this realization, he turns himself into the vessel of others' demands and expectations.

In the most immediate sense, Invisible Man feels himself the victim of these injunctions. They are, he tells us, "often in contradiction and even self contradictory" (2:19). Following them is suicidal. His efforts at being directed both perplex Invisible Man and make him feel torn apart inside. He does not know which set of injunctions to choose and has no basis for making the choice. His legacy appears to consist of two contradictory lines of advice, the first enigmatic and the second seemingly unambiguous. As a youth, Invisible Man witnesses his grandfather's death. The old man makes a final speech which Invisible Man's parents find more alarming than the fact of the old man's death. Invisible Man describes the scene:

78

he called my father to him and said, "Son, after I'm gone
I want you to keep up the good fight. I never told you, but
our life is a war and I have been a traitor all my born days,
a spy in the enemy's country ever since I gave up my gun
back in the Reconstruction. Live with your head in the lion's
mouth. I want you to overcome 'em with yesses, undermine
'em with grins, agree 'em to death and destruction, let 'em
swoller you till they vomit or bust wide open. (2:20)

This legacy leaves Invisible Man feeling confused and anxious. His grandfather had been, to all outward appearances,
"the meekest of men." Invisible Man understands neither how
this meekness is resistance nor how his own career of increasing acquiesence to and approval by the town's whites fits in
with his grandfather's injunction. It appears that Invisible Man
does not experience his grandfather's fierce determination to
fight the world. He visualizes himself, rather, "as a potential
Booker T. Washington." That is, he hopes to become the
model of what white people applaud blacks for: humble,
hardworking, respectable. To this end he seems willing to subjugate himself totally.

Invisible Man's outward behavior, like that of his parents
and his grandfather, is clearly reflective of the second line of
advice—the belief that one gives one's self over to those who
embody power, those who can bestow status and recognition.
"They" establish the rules by which one can achieve something. It is Invisible Man's role not to question these rules, but
only to adhere to them and compete by them to the best of
his ability.

We see his outward obedience to this principle in his graduation day address as a black boy in a southern town. He tells
us that he "delivered an oration in which I showed that humility was the secret, indeed, the very essence of progress . . .
Everyone praised me and I was invited to give the speech at
a gathering of the town's leading white citizens" (2:20–21).

When he arrives at the hotel to give this talk, he finds that

79

he must first take part in some preliminaries. He is ushered into the ballroom along with a number of other young negroes, the rest being a group of toughs. They are there, he is told, to provide the "entertainment" for this gathering of all the town's "big shots." The main event will be a "battle royal." All the boys are to be blindfolded and placed in a ring to fight it out, all against all, until only one boy is left standing. After changing into fighting clothes, they are led back into the main room to the yell of the school superintendent: "Bring up the little shines, gentlemen, bring up the little shines!" (2:22). Invisible Man is chagrined that the dignity of his speech may be impaired by the fighting, and is also "shocked to see some of the most important men in town quite tipsy. They were all there—bankers, lawyers, judges, doctors, fire chiefs, teachers, merchants. Even one of the more fashionable pastors" (2:22). This shock is not sufficient to prepare Invisible Man for the orgy of humiliation, lust, and violence which is to begin. The "leading citizens" first terrify and excite the boys (as well as themselves) through the sensuous dancing of a beautiful, nude blond. The men whip themselves into a virtual frenzy; they begin "reaching out to touch her" (2:23). A mad melee ensues as they get up and chase her, tossing her in the air "as college boys are tossed at a hazing." The woman's expression just before she escapes the mob reflects the situation. Invisible Man observes: "I saw the terror and disgust in her eyes, almost like my own terror" (2:24). He nonetheless proceeds with his part in the battle royal, feeling that his talk and its results will justify everything: "I wanted to deliver my speech more than anything in the world because I felt that only these men could truly judge my ability (2:28).

As he is reviled and threatened, blindfolded and beaten, his resolve to go on remains unshaken. As a reward for their efforts in the battle royal, Invisible Man and the others are told to pick up bills and gold coins which have been thrown onto a rug. As they lunge for the coins, they receive violent electric shocks. They boys are commanded to go on picking up the coins despite the pain. Spurred by their fear and greed, they proceed. Even this final touch does not deter Invisible Man from his goal. Yearning to express his humility and be judged, he struggles to the front of the audience, gulping down "blood, saliva and all . . . I spoke even louder in spite of the pain. But still they talked and still they laughed . . So I spoke with greater emotional emphasis. I closed my ears and swallowed blood until I was nauseated" (2:32).

The only intention Invisible Man can experience is to please these leaders with his message of humility. Yet he cannot help deviating from his script. Over and over, he talks of "social responsibility," meaning the expected passivity of blacks. As the men keep shouting at him to repeat, he transforms the phrase into "social equality," bringing the proceedings to a stunned halt. Surprised himself, Invisible Man dismisses his utterance as a slip of the tongue. He is correspondingly rewarded with a leather briefcase and "a scholarship to the state college for Negroes." Invisible Man "was overjoyed; I did not even mind when I discovered that the gold pieces I had scrambled for were brass pocket tokens" (2:34).

Consciously, Invisible Man feels "an importance," of which he had never dreamed. He feels, as the town's white leaders have told him, that he is starting on a path that will help shape the destiny of the black people. Only in his dreams does the true quality of his experience penetrate. That night, he dreams that his grandfather is telling him to open his briefcase. Inside, he discovers an engraved document saying, "To whom it may concern . . . Keep this Nigger-Boy Running" (2:35). He knows that he can be no more than a nigger-boy to the white culture, yet he yearns for their recognition. He knows that their gold is no more than brass tokens, and yet is overjoyed with their gifts and promises. Invisible Man is struggling to believe in the unbelievable, to revere the judges, doctors, and teachers who have revealed their bestiality. His is not simply a battle with reality, but with himself as well. Invisible Man works mightily to push away the "grandfather part" of himself, the part which impels him to see the unreality other men present to him and to reject it. Only at the end of his odyssey does he come to recognize the true source of his agony as being in himself: "I became ill of affirmation, of saying 'Yes' against the nay-saying of my stomach—not to mention my brain" (2:496). Indeed, Invisible Man can only bring himself to turn away from the dreams of others after repeated traumas, each serving to awaken him a little more. A central component of his initial project is to ignore both his stomach and his own perceptions, to plunge back into the dream at any price.

This project, and Invisible Man's unwilling tendency to disbelieve it, to negate it, are both manifest in his experiences at the Negro college. He provides a sardonic description of waiting in the college chapel on Founder's Day for the ritual service to begin:

> Here upon this stage the black rite of Horatio Alger was performed to God's own acting script, with millionaires come down to portray themselves; not merely acting out the myth of their goodness, and wealth and success and power and benevolence and authority in cardboard masks, but themselves, these virtues concretely! Not the wafer and the wine, but the flesh and the blood, vibrant and alive, and vibrant even when stooped, ancient and withered. (And who, in face of this, would not believe? Could even doubt?) (2:101)

Invisible Man wishes to be the black boy running after the myth he might become, the Horatio Alger or Booker T. Washington. He sees the performance of which he is a part as a ritual (as opposed to a reality?), but reveres it nonetheless. He wills himself to be a true believer. Invisible Man's goals have become most specific for him at college. They are embodied in the person of Dr. Bledsoe, the college president. Invisible Man describes him as "the example of everything I hoped to be: Influential with wealthy men all over the country; consulted in matters concerning the race; a leader of his people; the possessor of not one, but two Cadillacs, a good salary and a soft, good-looking and creamy-complexioned wife. What was more, while black and bald and everything white folks poked fun at, he had achieved power and authority; had, while black and wrinkle-headed, made himself of more importance in the world than most Southern white men. They could laugh at him but they couldn't ignore him" (2:101).

Recognition, comfort, and power are the rewards he seeks. If these require emasculating one's self, playing the black clown, Invisible Man is willing to pay the price. He can envision no destiny for himself outside of what the college, and all it represents, can grant to him. To reject what the college offers—the opportunity to be some version of Bledsoe—is to fall outside of history, to fall into the void. "And I remember, too, the talk of the visiting speakers, all eager to inform us of how fortunate we were to be a part of the 'vast' and formal ritual. How fortunate to belong to this family sheltered from those lost in ignorance and darkness" (2:101).

Thoroughly enmeshed in the ritual Bledsoe and the college represent, Invisible Man is eager to play the fawning servant for Mr. Norton, a wealthy, white trustee. Invisible Man is assigned to be Norton's driver during his annual visit to the campus. Simply feeling the power of this white man's car fills Invisible Man with pride and anxiety. He plays the sycophant; he feels it only natural to lie in order to please this aristocratic man. He expresses no shame at thus corrupting himself: "I knew . . . that it was advantageous to flatter rich white folks. Perhaps he'd give me a large tip, or a suit, or a scholarship next year" (2:39).

Yet the other side of Invisible Man continues to express its voice. Norton tells him that the black people are "somehow connected with my destiny." Invisible Man ponders this assertion but seems unable to accept it. Norton continues,

83

"Yes, you are my fate, young man. Only you can tell me what it really is. Do you understand?"

"I *think* I do, sir."

"I mean that upon you depends the outcome of the years I have spent in helping your school. That has been my life's work . . ." (2:42–43)

Norton is attempting to construct the school and all its graduates into a monument both to his own greatness and to his daughter. She had died as a young woman "too pure for life . . . too pure and too good and too beautiful." As Norton's part in the book unfolds, we are shown that his efforts represent both a denial and an enactment of his driving incestuous wishes. These desires, which he betrays but will not accept as his own, won't permit Norton to let his daughter die. Concomitantly, he cannot let either himself or others live in reality, but only as parts of his self-delusive dream. Norton goes on:

"So you see, young man, you are involved in my life quite intimately, even though you've never seen me before. You are bound to a great dream and to a beautiful monument. If you become a good farmer, a chef, a preacher, doctor, singer, mechanic—whatever you become, and even if you fail, you are my fate. And you must write me and tell me the outcome."

I was relieved to see him smiling through the mirror. My feelings were mixed. Was he kidding me? Was he talking to me like someone in a book just to see how I would take it? Or could it be, I was almost afraid to think, that this rich man was just the tiniest bit crazy? How could I tell him *his* fate? He raised his head and our eyes met for an instant in the glass, then I lowered mine to the blazing white line that divided the highway. (2:44)

Although Invisible Man senses Norton's madness, he is still unable to accept it. The resisting, critical part of himself still capable of stepping outside his dream is rejected as itself madness. In a beautifully drawn inversion, Ellison brings Invisible Man and Norton into contact with a group of "mad" veterans at the local bar and whorehouse. They are confronted by a black vet who is a former brain surgeon. This man represents a walking repudiation of their fantasies. He comes back to the South after his training and service in the army, the vet tells us, with the hope of saving life, "and I was refused . . . Ten men in masks drove out from the city at midnight and beat me with whips for saving a human life. And I was forced to the utmost degradation because I possessed skilled hands and the belief that my knowledge could bring me dignity" (2:88).

Invisible Man cannot comprehend or believe the vet. To hear what he says would destroy the fabric of Invisible Man's dream, the myth of what he wants to become. The vet, representing a dramatic externalization of the resisting part of the protagonist, accuses him directly:

> "You see," he said turning to Mr. Norton, "he has eyes and ears and a good distended African nose, but he fails to understand the simple facts of life. *Understand.* Understand? It's worse than that. He registers with his senses but short-circuits his brain. Nothing has meaning. He takes it in but he doesn't digest it. Already he is—well, bless my soul! Behold! a walking zombie! Already he's learned to repress not only his emotions but his humanity. He's invisible, a walking personification of the Negative, the most perfect achievement of your dreams, sir! The mechanical man!" (2:86)

The rest of the novel represents a series of movements toward and flights from the simple truth that the vet is expounding. In each such movement. Invisible Man gets increasingly in touch with his own anger, his own humanity and his own possibilities. He is expelled from school and humiliated by Bledsoe, who sends him to New York with false promises of help in finding employment and eventual readmission to college. Invisible Man finally comes to see that he has been deceived, and begins to awaken to his own feelings.

> Somewhere beneath the load of the emotion-freezing ice which my life had conditioned my brain to produce, a spot of black anger glowed and threw off a hot red light of such intensity that had Lord Kelvin known of its existence, he would have had to revise his measurements. A remote explosion had occurred somewhere, perhaps back at Emerson's or that night in Bledsoe's office, and it had caused the ice cap to melt and shift the slightest bit. But that bit, that fraction, was irrevocable. Coming to New York had perhaps been an unconscious attempt to keep the old freezing unit going, but it hadn't worked; hot water had gotten into its coils. Only a drop, perhaps, but that drop was the first wave of the deluge. (2:226)

He plunges back into another dream—of restorative social change—but the "remote explosion" continues to reverberate. He can no longer be totally the object in the dream of the other. Passion, anger, and his ability to phase into reality all interfere. He joins the "brotherhood," a white-led radical group, but never becomes totally a part of it. From the outset he is suspected of being too individualistic for their metaphor of all as one under an external will (ideology). As he is seduced by the wife of one of the brotherhood's white leaders, Invisible Man observes, "it was as though . . . the ideological was merely a superfluous veil for the real concerns of life" (2:363).

As the veil falls away, he discovers his own invisibility, discovers that other men identify him according to their own dreams and own needs rather than any quality he presents to them. This fills him with anguish but also propels him further and further in discovering possibility. The potential to exploit this invisibility, this refusal of other men to see reality, is personified by Rinehart, his hipster double.

As he wanders the streets of Harlem in a white hat and

sunglasses, he assumes Rinehart's identity in the eyes of those he meets. He is accosted by Rinehart's girl; by someone asking him to pull strings and get him a job; by someone who identifies Rinehart as a runner for the numbers game; by police for a payoff. Finally he picks up a handbill which reads in part:

> Behold the Invisible
> Thy will be done O Lord
> I see all, know all, tell all, cure all.
> You shall see the unknown wonders.
>> Rev. B. P. Rinehart
>> Spiritual technologist

He is near a store-front church, Rinehart's church:

Can it be, I thought, can it actually be? And I knew that it was. I had heard of it before but I'd never come so close. Still, could he be all of them: Rine the runner and Rine the gambler and Rine the briber and Rine the lover and Rinehart the Reverend? Could he himself be both rind and heart? What is real anyway? But how could I doubt it? He was a broad man, a man of parts who got around. Rinehart the rounder. It was true as I was true. His world was possibility and he knew it. He was years ahead of me and I was a fool. I must have been crazy and blind. The world in which we lived was without boundaries. A vast seething hot world of fluidity, and Rine the rascal was at home in it. It was unbelievable, but perhaps only the unbelievable could be believed. Perhaps the truth was always a lie. (2:430)

He was teetering precipitously on the edge of the void; confronting the allness that is nothingness.

You could actually make yourself anew. The notion was frightening, for now the world seemed to flow before my eyes. All boundaries down, freedom was not only the recognition of necessity, it was the recognition of possibility. And sitting there trembling I caught a brief glimpse of the possi-

bilities posed by Rinehart's multiple personalities and
turned away. It was too vast and confusing to contemplate.
(2:431)

He must pull back from the edge. He uses "Rinehart's truth"
to return substance to the world, giving it back its power over
him—its superintendency over his life—through the purpose
he assigns himself of seeking revenge on it for having lied to
him. His purpose would be the political murder of the human
sacrifice. He would fill the void with acts of destruction, fulfilling the command of his dying grandfather: "Live with your
head in the lion's mouth. I want you to overcome 'em . . ."

This phase, too, passes as Invisible Man rejects being the
huckster who exploits other men's madness. Caught in a race
riot that he has unwittingly helped to provoke, his project is
finally transformed. He no longer wishes to make history but
only aspires to the "stripping away of my illusionment" (2:
483). Closed in a manhole by a group of white looters, he
becomes delirious and has a dream that expresses his awakening. Invisible Man dreams that he is surrounded:

> the prisoner of a group consisting of Jack and old Emerson
> and Bledsoe and Norton and Ras and the school superin-
> tendent and a number of others whom I failed to recognize,
> but all of whom had run me, who now pressed around me
> as I lay beside a river of black water, near where an ar-
> mored bridge arched sharply away to where I could not see.
> And I was protesting their holding me and they were de-
> manding that I return to them and were annoyed with my
> refusal.
>
> "No," I said, "I'm through with all your illusions and
> lies, I'm through running."
>
> "Not quite," Jack said above the others' angry demands,
> "but you soon will be, unless you return. Refuse and we'll
> free you of your illusions all right."
>
> "No, thank you; I'll free myself," I said, struggling to
> rise from the cutting sand. (p. 492)

The men castrate him and then declare, "Now you're free of illusions . . . How does it feel to be free of one's illusions?"

> "Painful and empty," Invisible Man answers as he sees a glittering butterfly circle three times around my blood-red parts, up there beneath the bridge's high arch. "But look," I said pointing. And they looked and laughed, and suddenly seeing their satisfied faces and understanding, I gave a Bledsoe laugh, startling them. And Jack came forward, curious.
> "Why do you laugh?" he said.
> "Because at a price I now see that which I couldn't see," I said. (2:493)

Invisible Man has not acquired the capacity to see. He has transformed himself to the point where he can now accept that which he perceives and act upon it. One element of this action is negation, the refusal to accept the dreams of the other as reality. He chooses neither to be acquiescent to the dream nor to make its destruction his mission. The black militant, Ras the Exhorter, represents this latter possibility. As the race riot begins, Ras changes his title to "the Destroyer." Mounted on a black horse, he rides through Harlem armed with a spear and dressed like "an Abyssinian chieftan; a fur cap upon his head, his arm bearing a shield, a cape made of the skin of some wild animal around his shoulders" (2:481).

Ras's anger has helped to awaken Invisible Man, has made it easier for him to recognize the bad faith of the "brotherhood" and his own complicity in it. Yet he rebels at the possibility that Ras represents—of defining one's self by a mission of hatred and destruction. Invisible Man confronts Ras on the street and thinks to himself: "that I, a little black man with an assumed name should die because a big black man in his hatred and confusion over the nature of reality that seemed controlled solely by white men whom I knew to be as blind as he, was just too much, too outrageously absurd. And I knew that it was better to live out one's own absurdity than to die for that of others, whether for Ras's or Jack's" (2:484).

The problem that Invisible Man comes to experience is how one becomes his own self, comes to feel real and alive, becomes human. This is more a struggle with the self than with the world. As malignant as the dreams of others may be, one chooses the project of opposition to their dreams only at the cost of becoming a grotesque caricature like Ras. To become himself Invisible Man withdraws to his white cave, his undetected room in the tenement basement. It is only by thus isolating himself that he can overcome his sickness, his human weakness of re-enveloping himself in a new dream each time an old one crumbles.

> Well, now I've been trying to look through myself, and there's a risk in it. I was never more hated than when I tried to be honest. Or when, even as just now I've tried to articulate exactly what I felt to be the truth. No one was satisfied—not even I. On the other hand, I've never been more loved and appreciated than when I tried to "justify" and affirm someone's mistaken beliefs; or when I've tried to give my friends the incorrect, absurd answers they wished to hear. In my presence they could talk and agree with themselves, the world was nailed down, and they loved it. They received a feeling of security. But here was the rub: Too often, in order to justify *them*, I had to take myself by the throat and choke myself until my eyes bulged and my tongue hung out and wagged like the door of an empty house in a high wind. Oh, yes, it made them happy and it made me sick. (2:495–96)

In making this painful, terrifying step into isolation, Invisible Man discovers not the void, but himself. The perception he has tried so frantically to escape emerges, and he finds that he can live with it. "The fact is that you carry part of your sickness within you, at least I do as an invisible man. I carried my sickness and though for a long time I tried to place it in the outside world, the attempt to write it down shows me that at least half of it lay within me" (2:497–98). He sees that he can either continue to exist as a blind, invisible man in a world of dreams, or to seek something else. The alternative is not defined by its content; it is no specific project. It is, rather, the attempt to "burn out" one's "sickness . . . and go on to the next conflicting phase" (2:498). That phase beyond invisibility represents "an area in which a man's feelings are more rational than his mind" (2:496). Entering this area does not provide answers, but merely changes the terms of one's discourse with himself. As Invisible Man says, "it is precisely in that area that his will is pulled in several directions at one time."

Yet movement into this area of ambiguity, inner conflict and recognition of self represents the only significant move in his life. As a high school orator, the black Horatio Alger, as the social revolutionary, he has never been anything but "a material, a natural resource to be used" (2:439). By stepping outside of history, his "world has become one of infinite possibilities." He exhorts us that it's "a good view of life and a man shouldn't accept any other . . ." "Step outside the narrow borders of what men call reality and you step into chaos— ask Rinehart, he's a master of it—or imagination" (2:498).

Both Herzog and Invisible Man have denounced history in the quest to become more human. Their hibernations are not nihilistic; they do not represent surrender. They are, instead, a preparation. Only in isolation can they appreciate what they are and what they can be. This does not separate them from the world. It represents a new basis for contact with reality: "the world is just as concrete, ornery, vile and sublimely wonderful as before, only now I better understand my relation to it and it to me. I've come a long way . . ."

Each is left to define for himself the contents of his humanity, to know himself in his own terms. Their common struggle may, however, instruct us about the shared dilemmas of existence. Their anguish is not so different from that experienced by many. They felt unreal in their own existences and suffered the pain of choosing to make their lives real. This was not, for either of them, a choice that could be made once and then activated. It had to be made, negated and then reconfirmed. At each step, it became more fully experienced and less fearful. The terror that one would be suspended in a void should he leave the dream slowly dissipated as each man's experience, feelings, guilt, and imagination become more real to him. The space around them, they came to see, is never empty and never full except as they themselves fill it up or refuse to fill it.

The torment and partial awakening which Herzog and Invisible Man describe to us are dramatized, but are reflective of the inner struggles of real men. We see these struggles, in forms both eccentric and intolerable, in those whom we consider mad. It is in madness that we are confronted by man's unwillingness to become himself as the core of his existential dilemma. Freud was among the first to see and dramatize this issue in madness, and it is to him that we turn to explore the conflict further.

References

1. Saul Bellow, *Herzog*, New York, Viking Press (1961).
2. Ralph Ellison, *Invisible Man*, New York, Signet Books (1947).
3. Joseph Heller, *Catch 22*, New York, Dell (1961).

PART II
The Struggle To Flee the Self

4. Madness and Despair

> One might say perhaps that there lives not one single man who after all is not to some extent in despair, in whose inmost parts there does not dwell a disquietude, a perturbation, a discord, an anxious dread of unknown something, or of a something he does not even dare to make acquaintance with, dread of a possibility of life, or dread of himself. (4:155)

In this chapter we will try to fathom the desperation with which the self works to avoid being itself. Alienation tells us that this work of not being a self manifests itself in different modalities. The predominant modality is to plunge into culture, to become an imago that eschews being a self. In taking this path, the self joins forces with others equally desperate, others who reinforce the bad faith one is enacting. Another modality for fleeing the self is that particular state of being we once called "madness" but which we now know as psychopathology. The ancient figure of the madman, estranged from participating in the collective life, has become transposed into the figure of the psychiatric patient. The patient's experience parallels the experience of existence in culture. He experiences his being in the world as one of bondage and fraudulence. He fears that becoming himself is a danger to be avoided at all costs, and yet is tortured in his inability to be himself. If we are to better understand the maneuvers and assumptions of existence in culture as bad faith, a dialogue with the patient may be crucial. Indeed, our protagonists continually tell us, from their alienated stance, that life in culture represents a special kind of psychopathology: one endorsed by culture as sanity but knowable to the self as madness.

What compels us to open such a dialogue is that the patient is overtly despairing in the sense that he is grieving over his life, his own self. The patient, in his open search of a cure, highlights a process of self-examination or self-recrimination which men in culture generally strive to push away and ignore. Nonpatients, it would seem, experience many of these same issues but do not feel compelled to articulate and reveal their internal struggles. The self in culture recognizes the possibility of his own bad faith and the self-delusion it implies. But this perception is always tenuous and beclouded by the continuing acceptance of collective beliefs. Conformity to these beliefs excuses the self from questioning the meaningfulness of his own projects. In this context he sees such statements as Vonnegut's novels or Hoffman's street theater as diversions: statements of reality that he can play with but need not seriously consider. He can thus avoid a basic examination of the modalities and purposes of his own bad faith. To open a dialogue with the patient, to allow him to speak to us out of the peculiarities and particularities of his anguish, does not allow us to shrink from such an examination.

In conducting a dialogue with patients, we can hear, in some detail, the sequence of movement from being a self that is the agent of its own intentions, through negation of that self, to the restructuring of reality which the negation necessitates, to the sense of entrapment which this process engenders. The patient, like the despairer in culture, comes to feel futile and helpless in the face of outside forces, partially knowing that he has endowed these forces with the power to enslave him. More concretely, the patient illustrates for us the processes by which the self attempts to escape himself by generating particular ways of perceiving the world and himself, made manifest in a life script.

The patient separates his own actions from himself as intention, disowning responsibility for his being in the world. He flees his own impulses and desires, the signals from his stomach, by pretending that they don't exist. The patient empties himself of those things which give existence meaning and those aspects of himself that terrify him, projecting them on external objects. This transforms his internal struggle to be himself into an eternal battle with the world. The price for this transformation, this attempt to escape despair, is substantial. The patient continually re-encounters himself in the guise of malevolent others and is terrified by them. Part of the patient's terror, as we shall see, derives from the experience of internal impoverishment produced by projecting outside himself what it is that gives meaning to his existence. Another part of his terror, which seems to go along with the projective modality, is a magnification of what terrifies him about aspects of his own self. His own desires and impulses are reflected back to him in the form of hyperbole. Anger becomes the towering rage of a monster; desire confronts the self as unquenchable lust. The original intent of the symptom is to decrease anxiety, but the anxiety returns in new guises. Moreover, the patient must live with the self-estrangement and self-loathing of one whose whole existence is known to the self as a lie. The patient's plight is thus analogous to that of the despairing self in culture. Both the middle Americans and Invisible Man, we have seen, work mightily to separate themselves from their own actions. Like the patient, they assert that behavior and the self as the agent of its own intentions are independent of each other.

The psychotic patient, of course, demands precisely this exemption. He asserts that he must wash his hands eighty times a day or he will perish, that he must cover his tracks so the C.I.A. will not assasinate him. These things do not represent the kind of work that he would choose to do. They represent a calling; what calls him to do a work that he experiences as torturous is no less than the need to survive. It is such similarities between those in culture and those of the patient which make him both so disturbing and so instructive. If he can be deluded about the necessity of his acts, why not others also? This possibility can be particularly disturbing to men who must work to believe in their own rationality, who fight against the perception of their own futility. Goffman, Coles, Ellison and Bellow all testify that the struggle to believe in the authenticity of one's own being in the world is not confined within the walls of a psychiatric clinic.

It is here that alienation and madness coalesce in a way which resonates with the profound self doubts that pervade collective existence. Both the alienated and the patient declare that one's existence, one's perceptions, one's beliefs can become utterly alien to the self. One can live out an existence, only to awaken to the knowledge that it was all a sham, all useless. In a sense, the condition of patienthood is the most dramatic expression of this reversal. The patient needs and seeks a cure for precisely this sense of a life that is out of control because he cannot stop deluding himself about what he wants and needs. The psychotic patient demonstrates the human possibility of generating a reality—in the form of strange rules, other people's intentions, attenuated possibilities—which he then perceives as given to him with self-evident concreteness. The patient also demonstrates a capacity for lucidity, for recognizing this reality as a means he generates for fleeing from a self that is somehow intolerable to him.

The patient's anguish lies in his desperation to flee from recognition of this. Although he cannot escape from experiencing himself as possibility, he cannot accept what he is, what he does, or what he intends. He feels himself incapable of choice or action. Western culture has tended to flee from confronting the patient and the disturbing possibility he represents. The transposition from madness to patienthood has resulted in the situation, as Foucault puts it, in which "modern man no longer communicates with the madman: on one hand, the man of reason delegates the physician to madness, thereby authorizing a relation only through the abstract universality of disease; on the other, the man of madness communicates with society only by the intermediary of an equally abstract reason which is order, physical and moral constraint, the anonymous pressure of the group, the requirements of conformity. As for a common language, there is no such thing" (1:10). The experience of alienation reopens this negated dialogue with madness. The psychotic symptom can be seen as the analog of life in culture in that both are ways of fleeing from the self. Life as a cultural imago, like psychosis, can represent a negation of one's own agency. Both are built upon belief systems which fill reality with powerful, alien forces. Alienation represents itself as the analog of the psychotic's moments of lucidity. It represents the possibility of the self in culture awakening to own its self-deception.

It is in the realm of psychopathology that the modes of self-deception—attempts to escape from and redefine the self —have been most closely studied. Much of Freud's vocabulary, the major legacy of Western psychiatry, is a vocabulary of distortion and self-delusion. Such terms as repression, denial, conversion reaction, and paranoia are no more nor less than specific types of such distortion. Each represents a way in which one simultaneously negates an internal perception or experience while redefining external reality so as to support this original distortion of intent. Each symptom or "defense" also carries with it a built-in struggle. The self must work to maintain its own lie, which is always precarious. Each patient continues to know the truth even as he attempts to live out his self-deception and its attendant struggles. As we explore

99

the process by which such realities are constructed, defended, and lived with by madmen, we may know better how human beings generally respond to internal disquietude.

In the late nineteenth century, Freud, Breuer, Charcot, and others donned the white coat of medical science and listened to the life stories of malcontents, whose lives were a burden— a procedure that was regarded as mildly scandalous. Their very act implied belief in the reality of "inner disquietude." Doctors seemed to be saying that emotional anguish was just as real as sickness and death. The negative response to this position is still with us, and was highly manifest in the early years of psychoanalysis. The "analysts" (a name that came after the fact) not only listened to madmen and malingerers as if they were saying something coherent, but also had the audacity to claim that they were at the same time discovering truths about human functioning.[1]

Freud, in following the overt symptomatology of these early patients, emphasized sexual instincts as the issue over which the self was in conflict. In later formulations, sexuality and aggressiveness—both seen as representations of a yearning for release through death—were given equal value as the instinctual forces men sought to escape, control, and deny. Freud's doctrine of "instincts" is in no sense crucial, or even relevant, to the reading of Freud's case studies. It is the structure, not the content of the symptom that illuminates what alienation describes as the self's relation to the self and others as a desperate fleeing from itself. In this sense, the self's bad faith over its sexual interest is no different than bad faith over greed or lust for power or any other intent which a person may experience. It is the way in which the patients flee their own intentionality, only to re-experience it in new and grotesque forms, which is crucial.

There were two equally unique and significant features in Freud's early encounters with madness. The first was the peculiar picture or sense of self presented by the madmen. In the context of Victorian beliefs about man, they were puzzling and upsetting. The second peculiarity was in the quality of Freud's relation to them. He thought it worthwhile to listen to the nonsense they presented with the compulsive style of science. His willingness to take careful note of fantasies, misconstruals, desires, and fears of his patients (and later of himself and his colleagues) opened up a whole new universe to explore. The collective ignorance of this realm or layer of reality and the corresponding absence of any theory that could tell Freud what to look for, or how to understand what he found, led him to incredible efforts at simply gathering life stories. He later compared these self-explanations with his own experiences and concluded that they were prototypical of how men create their own realities and their own suffering. In the constant rehashing of Freud's specific metaphors and vocabulary, this very fundamental allegation remains unresolved and largely unexplored. His case studies are the starting point for his theoretical venture, and these patients exhibit the basic elements and paradoxes Freud wanted to resolve. In this chapter we will be concerned with exploring one of his most famous and rich clinical studies. The case represents the construction of a personal reality that was unaccaptable both to its author (the patient) and to his audience. In choosing this case of obsessional neurosis (in today's parlance, it would probably be designated as borderline schizophrenia) we will be dealing with much of the range of symptoms and complaints associated with insanity.

The case dates to 1909. Freud describes his first encounter with his young, university-educated patient. The young man complains of obsessions dating back to childhood which had become even more intense and troubling in the preceding four years. His major obsession was that some calamity would befall two loved ones, his father and his girl friend. The patient also reported an awareness of "compulsive impulses" to do such things as cut his own throat. He was further troubled by prohibitions that occasionally interfered with commonplace routines. Freud writes: "He had wasted years, he told me, in fighting against these ideas of his, and in this way had lost much ground in the course of his life" (3:19).

This young man was, in Freud's emerging categories, an obsessional neurotic. That is, he felt compelled to occupy his life with ideas and actions that were inexplicable and unacceptable to himself. The obsession is not simply a symptom from which the neurotic suffers. It is not the cause of his despair. To be an obsessional is to live in despair: to live as something other than "one's self," and to feel impotent to become one's self.

> The neurotic ceremonial [which the patient acts out] consists of little prescriptions, performances, restrictions and arrangements in certain activities of everyday life which have to be carried out always in the same or in a methodically varied way. These performances make the impression that they are mere "formalities"; they appear quite meaningless to us. Nor do they appear otherwise to the patient himself; yet he is quite incapable of renouncing them, for every neglect of the ceremonial is punished with the most intolerable anxiety, which forces him to perform it instantly . . . In slight cases the ceremonial appears to be only an exaggeration of an ordinary and justifiable orderliness, but the remarkable conscientiousness with which it is carried out, and the anxiety which follows its neglect, gives the ceremonial the character of a sacred rite. (2:26)

The young man under discussion—called the "rat man" because of one idea that plagued him—had exhibited an obsessional quality in his behavior since childhood. During his first hour of discussion with Freud, the patient describes events dating back to his fifth year. Having been allowed to finger and examine the genitals of a pretty young governess, he was "left with a burning and tormenting curiosity to see the female body" (3:21).

The rat man's precocity may not be surprising, but his reaction to it was somewhat strange. He said to Freud: "When I was six years old I already suffered from erections, and I know that once I went to my mother to complain about them" (3:22). The patient had thus transformed a pleasurable excitation into an affliction from which he "suffered." He makes a further connection between his sexual interests and the development of

> a morbid idea that my parents knew my thoughts; I explained this to myself by supposing that I had spoken them out loud, without having heard myself do it. I look on this as the beginning of my illness. There were certain people, girls, who pleased me very much, and I had a very strong wish to see them naked. But in wishing this I had an uncanny feeling, as though something must happen if I thought such things, and as though I must do all sorts of things to prevent it.
>
> (In reply to a question he gave an example of these fears: "For instance, that my father might die"). Thoughts about my father's death occupied my mind from a very early age and for a long period of time, and greatly depressed me. (3:22-23)

This state of affairs, as Freud points out, contains the same basic components as the other uncanny and painful situations the patient experiences as he grows older. There is a wish or a desire of conjuring up a pleasurable situation (seeing and examining women). The wish could not, however, be simply accepted and acted upon. Instead, unpleasant consequences come to be associated with the wish, as well as "painful affect" (3:23). The patient is, at this early age, experiencing his relation to himself and to his world as problematic. Remarkably, problems are not "happening" to him, he is conjuring them up. He is creating a world in which parents hear his thoughts. He even mentions the possibility of speaking his thoughts aloud if necessary, precisely so that the parents will know them, and yet describes this possibility as "morbid."

The world he "sees" is full of obstacles to enjoyment. A universe of choice and plenty, filled with highly aroused young frauleins anxious to seek mutual pleasure, has become a moral universe. His father's death gets established as the price the patient must pay for his desires. As we will see shortly, the connection the patient draws between his father's death and pleasurable acts becomes more complicated—that is, despite the patient's protestations, the father's death itself is not a totally abhorrent outcome.

Although the perceptions of being overheard and the vision of the father's death had an uncanny quality, they nonetheless impinged on the patient as any perceived reality might. To the observer it was patently obvious that the rat man was fabricating his environment. Yet nowhere does the patient report this feeling.

The symptoms of adulthood share this quality: the patient is distressed by his own fantasies, which he cannot control and which he regards with complete seriousness. His fantasies are events that he feels are happening to him. His "great obsessive fear" revolved around a story told by a fellow officer during military maneuvers. The patient had the greatest difficulty in bringing himself to repeat the details to Freud, and does so in a strangulated fashion. It has to do with a rumored Eastern torture in which a "criminal was tied . . . a pot was turned upside down . . . some rats were put into it . . , and they . . . bored their way in" to his anus. Freud remarks on the strangeness of the rat man's facial expression while relating this material. He describes this expression as "horror at pleasure of his own of which he himself was unaware." The patient proceeded with the greatest difficulty: "At that moment the idea flashed through my mind that this was happening to a person who was very dear to me" (3:27). He envisions this torture being applied to the women he hopes to marry. In the most immediate sense the patient is a passive onlooker to the event. That is, he did not fantasize himself applying the torture; "it was being carried out as it were impersonally" (3:27). Several moments later the patient also reveals to Freud that he has the same fantasy in relation to a second person, his father. This is perhaps even more peculiar, since his father had died several years earlier. And yet the patient is afraid. He even feels compelled to take action to prevent the atrocity. In telling the story to Freud, he interrupts himself in order to assure the therapist that he himself finds "these thoughts entirely foreign and repugnant" (3:27). Then rat man also tells Freud that these thoughts rush into his mind with great rapidity, almost as if they present themselves simultaneously. Part of this same rush of ideas was a "sanction" or ritual measure which the rat man felt he had to adopt lest his forebodings (which were vivid) come true.

The measure that wards off the torture is verbal. The rat man safe-guards his loved ones, both living and deceased, by saying, "But, whatever are you thinking," simultaneously making a "gesture of repudiation" (3:28).

The patient is not simply seeing the world in a way that Freud cannot endorse. He is absurd to himself, creating paradoxes within his own structure of reality. The rat man is embarrassed about his fears. He knows that his father is dead and beyond harm, yet the idea of his torture and the fear persist. To defend against these ideas, the patient shifts his perspective, admitting possibilities alien to his beliefs. Having repudiated religion during adolescence, he nonetheless raises the possibility of punishment in "eternity-to the next world" (3:30). Freud comments that the rat man had, at this point, "reconciled his beliefs and obsessions by saying to himself: 'What do you know about the next world? Nothing can be known about it. You're not risking anything—so do it' " (3:30). This statement is itself paradoxical. On the one hand, it justifies belief in the possibility that the father is still available for punishment in the hereafter. The term "punishment" also raises new connotations. The father (and perhaps the lady by implication) would not be suffering gratuitous torture; punishment implies retribution for an earlier misdeed.

The patient does not, however, allude to what the father has "done wrong." The last sentence of the statement "You're not risking anything—so do it" implies that the patient, as concerns himself, repudiates the possibility of an afterlife. The rat man can do "it" (whatever that might be) with impunity. These contradictions are produced by a person who "in other respect is particularly clear-headed" (3:30). We might reasonably assume that the contradictions have a meaning and a purpose, are not simply reflective of some intellectual impairment. More generally, we can say that basic elements of the obsessive condition reappear in newer and more elaborate guises. The patient becomes absurd to himself in strange efforts to forestall a calamity that is unreal, impossible. If any one obsession represents the patient's "major presenting symptom," it is as follows: The evening after the rat man had first heard the torture described, he reports that the same captain who had told the story had given him a package. The captain had explained that "Lieutenant A has paid the charges for you. You must pay him back." The package contained eyeglasses that the rat man had ordered. Upon hearing the captain's words, however, he became preoccupied with a "sanction." He feared that if he repaid the money, the rat torture would be applied to his father and girl friend. In the same rush of ideas, a counterinjunction occurs to him: "You must pay back the 3.80 crowns to Lieutenant A" (3:28). These words had formed on his lips, spoken half aloud.

A further element now becomes apparent. Although the patient has devised a means of warding off the impending tragedy, he struggles mightily with the issue of whether he will avail himself of it. He can default on his debt to protect those dear to him, and yet he feels that he cannot default. At the same time, he sets up obstacles to carrying out his counterinjunction (i.e., defaulting). He finds reasons not to repay the "loan."

Two days after these ideas had occurred to the patient, the army maneuvers were drawing to a close. He had spent the subsequent period attempting to repay Lieutenant A, but new circumstances kept getting in the way. Freud reports:

> First he had tried to effect the payment through another officer who had been going to the post office. But he had been much relieved when this officer brought him back the money, saying that he had not met Lieutenant A there, for this method of fulfilling his vow had not satisfied him, as it did not correspond with the wording, which ran: "*You* must pay back the money to Lieutenant A." Finally, he had met Lieutenant A, the person he was looking for; but he had refused to accept the money, declaring that he had not paid anything for him, and had nothing whatever to do with the post, which was the business of Lieutenant B. This had thrown my patient into great perplexity, for it meant that he was unable to keep his vow, since it had been based upon false premises. He had excogitated a very curious means of getting out of his difficulty, namely that he should go to the post office with both men, A. and B., that A. should give the young lady there the 3.80 crowns, that the young lady should give them to B., and that then he himself should pay back the 3.80 crown to A. according to the wording of his vow. (3:29)

We see in the patient a man suspended in conflict. He can neither act effectively nor decline action. The rat man must strive to achieve the ridiculous, and create conditions in which this striving falls short. And yet these struggles feel real to the patient; it is his "normal" life which does not.

That evening—as the struggle over how and whether to repay A rages on in the patient—he is required to attend a final gathering of the officers before the maneuvers end. "It had fallen to him to reply to the toast of 'The Gentlemen of the Reserve.' He spoke well, but *as if he were in a dream*, for at the back of his mind he was being incessantly tormented by his vow" (3:30, italics added). The level of shared or cultural reality is misty and unsubstantial to the rat man;

his fears and fantasies at least have emotional vividness.

He continues to assume that he will follow the injunction and repay the money, and develops a complicated plan of juggling train schedules, allowing him both to give the funds to A and return to Vienna. Yet he is resistant to following through on his plan and possibly "cutting a foolish figure." The dilemma is experienced as complete. Arguments favoring the alternative of paying are "evenly balanced" (3:31) with the alternative of not paying A the money. Regarding the "even balance" as an element of reality (not something he has created), the patient follows an established practice of allowing "his actions to be decided by chance events as though by the hand of God" (3:31). Thus when a porter inquires if he is planning to take the ten o'clock train, he takes this as a sign indicating the course he must take. Feeling that the decision has been made for him, the patient is "greatly relieved" (3:31).

The blurring of boundaries, and confusion over the source of action or agency, is as noteworthy as the content of the rat man's ideas. He experiences himself as responding, as following external directives that leave him no choice. He does not think of himself as interpreting the porter's question as a signal to take a certain train. For the patient the question *means* he should get on the train. In the course of his journey, he continues to act out an equivalent, futile drama. At each station, he considers getting off and returning to carry out his vow. He is, however, "prevented" from turning back by a variety of "circumstances": he has reserved a table for lunch, he has relatives living near one of the stations, and so on. In this manner he moves further and further away from the possibility of fulfilling his pledge; yet he continues to explain his actions as if he indeed planned to return to the site of the maneuvers.

The rat man arrives in Vienna, seeks out his friend, and lays the matter before him. The patient comes to the realization that he owes the money for his glasses to a young lady employed at the post office, not to one of the officers. More-over, the patient recollects that he had known this fact for some time, even before meeting the captain. Despite the fact that he has cleared up his "misunderstanding," he experiences a resurgence of his obsession. He resolves to see a physician. His "intent," as he recognizes it, is to obtain a medical certificate telling Lieutentant A that he must accept money from the patient. When he actually arrives at Freud's office, his goal has changed: he asks "to be freed of his obsessions" (3:33).

Like his sexuality, the rat man feels his obsession to be both a burden and something he is unwilling to give up. The obsession has meaning for him, Freud discovers, because of what it symbolizes. Moreover, this symbolic content is, on the most immediate level, as mysterious to the patient as it is to Freud.

Gradually, a number of associations to the rat idea are produced. The imagined torture, the patient comes to realize, is sexual as well as sadistic. The rat boring his way into the body of the victim is associated with a penis and, with anal intercourse. At the same time, the patient associates rats with feces and with disease. A number of verbal slips and ritual sayings also indicate that he thinks of rats as equivalent to money or wealth. Finally, early childhood memories (or cur-rent fantasies disguised as such) create a link between the idea of the rat and that of children. Even more specifically, he identifies himself with the sharp-toothed, devouring rat.

The patient is interposing symbols between himself and his own desires, his own body, his own qualities of being. The symbols he chooses are at once grotesque and liberating. Through them he acts as the not self, hating and disowning his (imagined) actions while reveling in them. The obsession is the scenario for a fantasy which the patient continually reenacts. The scenario is a shifting one but is always con-stituted of the same few elements and has a common out-come. The outcome is that nothing ever happens.

As Freud remarks, the madman "suffers from memories." In this particular instance, the rat man has equated the captain with his own father. He had re-experienced himself as an omnipotent child—whose very thoughts are deadly—confronting a cruelly punishing parent. He begins living in the obsession with this self-designated role. Simultaneously, a contradictory theme is being played out. As in the other spheres of his life, the patient partially identifies with the father—that is, with the role of torturer. He also identifies himself, obversely, as his father's slave. The patient is at once his father's victim and his tormentor. The rat man feels incapable of ignoring the captain's (parental) injunction to repay the money, even though he "knows" the captain to be in error. He cannot even bring himself to tell the captain he is wrong. He is servile to the older man's will. It is the patient's "loved ones" who are subjected to heinous torture, thus victimizing the patient himself with unendurable suffering. At the same time, we cannot but observe that it is the rat man who has created the imagined situation of his father's destruction. The victim becomes victimizer, finding both suffering and pleasure in each role. The patient has split both himself and his father into symbols that act out different aspects of this internal drama.

In the fantasies he creates for himself, the rat man experiences two poles of possibility: exquisite power and exquisite vulnerability or helplessness. Yet he can choose neither, so cannot fully identify with any role in the script. Thus there can be no outcome or resolution in the obsessional story. No one element can triumph and be brought to actuality. All remain in the purgatory of potential, vivid enough to titillate renounced desires, none real enough to permit consummation. The patient refuses to become the father, the father's chattel, or himself. His fantasies do not even admit this latter alternative, which appears to be totally beyond his power to imagine.

Freud argues that the patient's illness permits him to avoid choice, to avoid becoming either like his father or like the rebellious slave. In what we would call his real existence, the patient had the opportunity of marrying a wealthy cousin. He feels torn between this alternative and that of pursuing the impoverished woman he loves. Marrying the cousin would ensure financial prosperity, but he is unable to renounce his fiancée. The issue is further complicated by the patient's remembrance of his father's history. That is, the father was faced by a similar choice in his youth and married the girl with money.

In his own perception, following the same course would make the patient a "good boy," would make him his father's agent. Conversely, selecting the improvished fiancée was experienced as a violation of his father's injunction. The choice between two women had been translated into a conflict "between his [the patient's] love and the persisting influence of his father's wishes" (3:56). We must note both that the father is deceased and that he could have expressed no opinion on the dilemma, since it did not exist in the father's lifetime.[2] The patient is conflicted about violating the presumed wishes of an imago: the dead father.

The meaning or purpose of the conflict, as Freud remarks, can be inferred from its consequences. In this case, "by falling ill [the rat man] avoided the task of resolving [his conflict] in real life . . . [T]he chief result of his illness was an obstinate incapacity for work, which allowed him to postpone the completion of his education for years" (3:57).

The patient acts as if he cannot act because of conflicting loyalties, and because of unreconcilable demands from the outer world. We can hear his problem quite differently. The patient is himself composing the demands and counter demands that he subsequently feels are tearing him apart. In the universe the rat man has created for himself, there can be no satisfying action without penalty. He reports to Freud, for example, that "several years after his father's death, the first time he experienced the pleasurable sensations of copulation, an idea sprang into his mind: This is glorious! One might murder one's father for this" (3:59). Why, we might wonder, would one have to.

Just as in his childhood, the patient creates the conditions whereby he inhibits his own pleasure. His very choice of a love object—his fiancée—evidences this characteristic as clearly as his "symptoms." Early in adulthood he fixed upon this particular woman, although knowing that "financial obstacles made it impossible to think of an alliance with her" (3:38). His aim is thus inhibited as it is generated: he has selected a woman he cannot possess. We also know that he has selected a woman who does not choose to marry him, and who carries on with other loyalties and friendships to a degree that torments him.

This grand passion for his lady is inhibited in another way. He "had loved her very much, but he had never felt sensual wishes towards her, such as he had constantly had in his childhood" (3:41). A great deal "stands between" the patient and what we might regard as erotic or interpersonal fulfillment. He spends his life pursuing a woman he cannot afford, who does not want him, and for whom he feels no sensual desire. In fact, the alliance itself was apparently being questioned. When the patient had gone on maneuvers, "there had been a certain coolness between himself and his lady . . . his doubts as to his lady's merits had increased" (3:75). We might infer that consummation is not highly probable.

The patient, however, still regards himself as being in hot pursuit of the woman. We know that he had, earlier in the interminable courtship, conceived of a peculiar mechanism for breaking the impasse. This idea was "his father's death might make him rich enough to marry her" (3:38). He immediately repents for this thought, "wishing that his father might leave him nothing at all" (3:38). Another obstacle is added to the list. For the patient, gaining his impossible object has been linked to terrible loss (the father) and unbearable guilt. The central project for the patient is winning his fiancé. His relation to the project is this: he is chasing something he does not really want, against impossible obstacles, and if he succeeds, he will pay a terrible price.

The pattern is a familiar one in the rat man's life. We have heard of the early childhood misadventures, and others followed. At age 12 he fell in love with a little girl. His love, as he describes it, "had not been sensual," and she also "had not shown him as much affection as he had desired" (3:38). His father's demise is once again established as the mechanism for overcoming his difficulties. The patient is struck by the idea that the little girl would be kind to him in the event of a misfortune, and "as an instance of such a misfortune his father's death had forced itself upon his mind." In this context, too, the death idea is abhorrent to him and is "energetically repudiated."

With incredible consistency the patient finds ways to demolish the pathways to his own pleasure. He finds women who will not return his love, and works hard to avoid those who might. We hear little about the wife who has been offered to him, but we are told that she was "lovely, rich and well connected," so that marrying into the family "would offer him a brilliant opening in his profession" (3:56). The rat man offers little evidence of interest in these bounties.

Even when his interest is aroused and the prospect of more casual pleasure is raised, the patient finds a means of backing off. We have been told that the patient was aware that a girl at the post office had paid for his glasses, and he also reveals to Freud that she had at the same time made "a complimentary remark about himself" (3:67). In this context he also indicates:

> that the landlord of the inn at the little place where the
> post office was had a pretty daughter. She had been
> decidedly encouraging to the smart young officer, so that he
> had thought of returning there after the maneuvers were
> over and of trying his luck with her. Now, however, she
> had a rival in the shape of the young lady at the post office.

Like his father in the tale of his marriage, he could afford now to hesitate upon which of the two he should bestow his favours when he had finished his military service. We can see at once that his singular indecision whether he should travel to Vienna or go back to the place where the post office was, and the constant temptation he felt to turn back while he was on the journey were not so senseless as they seemed to us at first. To his conscious mind, the attraction exercised upon him by Z———, the place where the post office was, was explained by the necessity for seeing Lieutenant A and fulfilling the vow with his assistance. (3:68)

We can also note that the patient travels on all the way to Vienna. He feels unable to decide between two attractive, available young ladies, or to decide to pursue them both. Instead, he surrounds his apparent feelings of indecision with a ridiculous fabrication about indebtedness, and "resolves" matters by distancing himself from both of the attractive girls.

We have now seen four instances of a common scenario. At ages 5 and 12 and twice in his young adulthood, the rat man has been involved in unfulfilled passions. At each instance he experiences his inability to achieve gratification as externally caused. He is, in fact, willing to "read" outer reality in whatever way necessary to coincide with this belief. These distortions or choices of how to regard the world are so blatant that we might infer that the patient has chosen to be involved in unconsummated flirtations. It is difficult, however, to disregard the contradictory evidence. The rat man declares a need for the objects he selects, and indeed suffers when separated from them. He is not simply playing at being the thwarted or rejected suitor, he is experiencing the torments of the role. At the same time, he is remarkably inventive at finding new ways to occupy the same anguished state.

The rat man's relation to the paternal imago (living and dead) can now be seen as one of several devices he utilizes toward a common end: escape from gratification. The patient has constructed his world along the lines of a nightmare. No matter what is made available to him, he wants something else. That which he wants is always to be withheld, and protected by unconquerable monsters. The patient betrays his own ends in his love of these very monsters. He even resurrects them when they die. His father, in this sense, has or had no independent existence in the world. For the patient, the father is part of the self. The rat man wills his father into and out of existence as suits his purpose. He constitutes the father in the same way he constitutes his friends, enemies, and a-mours: endowing them with feelings, intentions, and abilities that coincide with the patient's dramaturgical needs. There is no experiential demarcation between the patient and the world that surrounds him. Stimuli from that world take on special meanings. The "rules" of transformation he uses in endowing these meanings relate to internal convenience. The shape of the drama—the patient's struggle against a bounteous but withholding environment—is the given. All perceptions of reality are controlled by and flow from it. The paternal imago has particular uses in the rat man's drama but ultimately is experienced in the same way as the self. That is, he loves the father with narcissistic tenacity, and feels an overwhelming desire to destroy him. The patient evidences this same conflict about his own being:

> One day while he was away on his summer holidays the idea suddenly occurred to him that he was too fat [German *dick*] and that he *must make himself thinner*. So he began getting up from table before the pudding came round and tearing along the road without a hat in the blazing heat of an August sun. Then he would dash up a mountain at the double, till, dripping with perspiration, he was forced to come to a stop. On one occasion his suicidal intentions actually emerged without any disguise from behind this mania for getting thinner: as he was standing

on the edge of a steep precipice he suddenly received a command to jump over, which would have been certain death. (3:47)

Narcissism and self-obliteration intertwine; the drive to purify, to turn one's self into the perfect being, leads to the precipice. But the rat man can choose neither to live as he is nor to jump.

This turbulent, painful paralysis is a basic condition of existence for him. He attempts to cast the world in terms that justify and make the condition endurable. In constituting a world of monsters, the patient strives to empty himself of the most prominent elements of his being: passion, hatred, and the will to immobilize himself. In the composition the rat man lives out, he seeks "love" without desire, is innocent of the suffering inflicted upon others, and could surely act "if only" reality would stop inhibiting him. He experiences his life as inhibited and predetermined by every conceivable element in the universe. A casual story told by a fellow officer, a porter's question at a railway station, or his fiancée's attachment to her relations are all experienced as overwhelming events. The patient asks to be freed from these constraints and misfortunes, but he asks in a passive voice. He acts in bad faith, projecting the notion that he is the unwilling victim of reality. He cannot admit, or even experience, his collaboration in defining and creating the reality which oppresses him.

At the same time, he is capable of moments of lucidity, transformation, awakening. Freud and the patient's friend in Vienna can only help the rat man to disentangle his strange creations because the patient himself provides the data. In the obsessive dream he is living out, he continually bemoans his destiny. When awake, he struggles against the dreaming process itself. He is not entirely immersed in his madness. He struggles to repudiate it, to live outside of the monotonic script. This struggle, too, is in bad faith. In labeling the obsessions "things" from which he is to be "freed," he is treating his own behavior, conflicts, and tensions as the not me. His request for cure is ambivalent. To be cured, in the terms he envisions, is to empty the self, to declare one's own being null and void.

The request for therapy, like the other concerns in the patient's life, is the quest for an endless heroic struggle. He challenges Freud to enslave him, and fights to avoid enslavement. He uses Freud as another demon he must (but cannot) resist and conquer. Freud writes:

> There came an obscure and difficult period in the treatment; eventually it turned out that he had once met a young girl on the stairs in my house and had on the spot promoted her into being my daughter. She had pleased him, and he pictured to himself that the only reason I was so kind and incredibly patient with him was that I wanted to have him for a son-in-law. At the same time he raised the wealth and position of my family to a level which agreed with the model he had in mind. But his undying love for his lady fought against the temptation. After we had gone through a series of the severest resistances and bitterest vituperations on his part, he could no longer remain blind to the transference phantasy and the actual state of affairs in the past. I will repeat one of the dreams which he had at this period, so as to give an example of his manner of treating the subject. He dreamed that *he saw my daughter in front of him with two patches of dung instead of eyes . . . he was marrying my daughter not for her "beaux yeux" but for her money.* (3:57–58)

The patient experiences Freud as trying to entrap him, possess him as a son-in-law. To do this, Freud uses his paternal strength (wealth, status) to purchase him. This involves an interesting reversal. The patient, in his fantasy, is acting under the assumption that he is valuable. It is Freud, through his daughter, who evokes contempt. The fantasized relationship is a mutual rip-off. Freud seeks to rob the patient of his independence, his self. The patient is hustling Freud for his daughter and money. The master-slave game is being played out on two different levels.

Freud reports:

> Things soon reached a point at which, in his dreams, his waking phantasies, and his associations, he [the patient] began heaping the grossest and filthest abuse upon me and my family, though in his deliberate actions he never treated me with anything but the greatest respect. His demeanour as he repeated these insults to me was that of a man in despair. "How can a gentleman like you, sir," he used to ask, "let yourself be abused in this way by a low, good-for-nothing wretch like me? You ought to turn me out: that's all I deserve." While he talked like this, he would get up from the sofa and roam about the room—a habit which he explained at first as being due to delicacy of feeling: he could not bring himself, he said, to utter such horrible things while he was lying there so comfortably. But soon he himself found a more cogent explanation, namely, that he was avoiding my proximity for fear of my giving him a beating. If he stayed on the sofa he behaved like some one in desperate terror trying to save himself from castigations of boundless dimensions . . . (3:65)

Each act is the negation of that which precedes it. The declaration of unworthiness is embedded in a context of narcissistic grandeur. In subjecting the therapist to such vituperation, the patient expresses his ambivalence toward himself. He is uncertain whether the world is too vile to be worthy of him, or he is himself too vile to be worthy of living in the world. This uncertainty can be seen as linked to another conflict. The patient cannot decide how to feel about what is inside himself—the desire to punish or be punished, to receive or withhold gratification. To escape this confusion and agony, he empties himself of hatred, experiencing it as coming from others (for example, from Freud in the anticipated "beating" or "castigations of boundless dimensions"). The patient strives to structure the therapeutic interaction so that it will provide gratification in two ways. First, he casts himself as the little boy or peasant playing opposite Freud's stern patriarch. This frees him to express his rage against the unassailable object, and to feel inhibited by an outer force. It also relieves guilt, putting him in the position of victim or slave, thus providing the right to "strike back." The aggressive thoughts toward father, Freud, and girl friend are all "justified" by the patient's feeling of being the aggrieved party, the one who is having his life taken away from him.

In this context, the patient acts out the dominant, sadistic role. He steals back that which is rightfully his: In taking Freud's daughter and money, or killing his father for his estate, he acts as if he can retrieve a sense of worth and potency. Within the drama, interchange between self and others is mutual theft. Wealth and potency must always be achieved at the other's expense. Both role images (thief and victim) are unbearable. Neither player can act as himself and for himself, but only through the medium of stolen goods.

The world experienced by the rat man is divided into the crippled and the fraudulent. The image of cripple or the incomplete, we might infer, is related to the patient's continual separation of parts of himself. He repeatedly disowns his intentions and feelings, encountering them with shock and fear as he wanders in the world (the captain's sadism, Freud's aggressiveness). He feels servile to their presence in the universe, but at the same time knows their unreality. The cripple knows himself as a fraud.

The rat man feels compelled to become a patient. That is, he asks others to free him from his affliction. This request is in bad faith: he asks others to free him from himself, but the scenario is already written. No movement will be allowed to take place. The would-be therapist will become the enemy and the rejected savior. He rejects the longed-for possibility of abandoning the drama as a threatening, alien idea. He stands poised between the agony of living out his own metaphor and the terror of abandoning it.

In this the rat man is not really different either from other patients or from those who find themselves living an alienated existence in culture; he stands out only because of the peculiar *content* by which he expresses his conflict over his self and his desires. The outline of this struggle is all too familiar. Each of Freud's patients, like Vonnegut's protagonists and the people that Cleaver, Hoffman and Coles encounter, is riddled by impulses, longings, and self-perceptions that are regarded as abhorrent. Each goes to enormous lengths to deny these perceptions, to transform them and escape to a self-deception that protects the self from these intrusions. Each continues to struggle with the issue of the viability of the self-deception, not knowing whether it is another affliction or the only possible cure for his dis-ease.

The rat man, like despairers in culture, has construed his world to be a nightmarish battle where others are out to debase and destroy him. He, too, launches into the project of combating these villains. He vacillates between seeing himself as incredibly good and valuable and experiencing himself as vile and debased. He is, however, always innocent. He claims hostility toward neither his father nor his fiancée, and no guilt for his fantasies of torture.

The rat man is always innocent because he never selects his own course of action. He simply adheres to moral injunctions and the demands of "reality." The porter's inquiry and the "voice of God" serve the same function. They separate action from intention; they make action servitude. The rat man creates his convoluted scenarios after adopting a given premise, which is a refusal to accept his own desires. He struggles to avoid acting out his lascivious intentions toward women: equally he flees a desire to inflict pain on his father. The creations and distortions that follow enable him to maintain the illusion of never having felt these desires, or having been forcefully separated from them. His striving is subsequently carried on in the mode of bad faith. He sees his wishes enacted, but only as a victim or passive onlooker. Having renounced his intentions, he subsequently creates realities that "push" him toward these disowned proclivities. In this transformation he is made to feel persecuted and helpless. His behavior becomes alien to his sense of his own being. The patient struggles with the issue of his own sense of agency. Unable to face that struggle, he works to manage his despair by making his own agency an issue between himself and others. The others are seen as the appropriators of his agency, and he must do battle with them until he reappropriates what was stolen from him. The patient lives out endless metaphors that are the transformations of this single set of themes—the hunter and the hunted; the victim and the victimizer; the fox and the hounds.

It is a terrible work, for the patient must empty himself of his experiences of being the agent of his possibilities— whether sexual or otherwise. He tries to manage the despair he experiences over being a self by surrendering everything to the work of inventing and sustaining an absolute certainty: his suffering is not within him but is imposed on him by monstrous and grotesque things. Everything visible must bear witness to this—at precisely the moment he is the hunter, he must also be the prey; and at precisely the moment he is the prey, he must be the hunter. The circle must not open for an instant. The stakes of the game, for him, are everything—to keep his despair within a dream.

Our protagonist works to create or maintain his own misery. The patient reshapes and redefines the bits and pieces of his environment to create an oppressive reality. He subsequently longs to be set free from this prison. We can see him as the prisoner of his own scenario, just as he occasionally expresses disbelief about his own productions.

The pattern of negating desire, claiming perfect innocence, and feeling surrounded by evil doers goes beyond the narrow confines of madness. This negation of self, the feeling of being forced by reality to act as one does, is the hallmark of both madness and bad faith, the latter representing the basic pattern of being in culture. The patient's claims of victimization and servitude are dismissed as mad because they are idiosyncratic. Culture, on the other hand, declares acceptable premises for how and why one can feel victimized and enslaved. These explanations represent the collective scenario for eternal despair. If we could abstract ourselves from these rules—as we demand that patients denounce their symptoms—these patterns might become more manifest to us. The "sane," we will attempt to demonstrate in greater detail, also enslave and disown their selves. They do this through the process of adapting to culture just as surely as the rat man did it by withdrawing into a personal reality. Moreover, this movement into the collective myth is spurred by the same problem the rat man struggles with: the unwillingness of the self to know and live with its own proclivities. This refusal of selfhood and agency leads to a sense of being in eternal purgatory.

References

1. Michael Foucault, *Madness and Civilization*, New York, Pantheon Books (1965).
2. Sigmund Freud, *Obsessive Acts and Religious Practices*, Vol. 2 of Collected Papers, New York, Basic Books (1959).
3. Sigmund Freud, *Three Case Histories*, New York, Collier Books (1963).
4. Soren Kierkegaard, *The Sickness unto Death*, Princeton, N.J., Princeton University Press (1968).

5. Myth and Culture

To this point we have been dealing essentially with the individual in his struggles to relate to himself and to a larger culture. In the process of this struggle the self can become estranged from its own life and its own productions. One comes to see his existence as absurd and bogus. This sense of estrangement from one's self is clearly manifest in madness. The very word "schizophrenia," which has become the symbol for madness in our age, is a reference to such internal warfare.

The sense of alienation in culture points to another condition in which a person may feel equally divided and false. "Sanity," as defined by our culture, is seen as no more than a special case of madness, the symptoms of which are in accordance with cultural dicta. Moreover, this separation from self which culture represents can be seen to exhibit the same underlying form as the "symptoms" of Freud's patients. The symptom and the culture structure "reality" in the same way: both create a world in which necessary objects or qualities reside in some space outside the self, which must then embark on the mission of gaining these things (be they nurturance, strength, or protection) in order to feel some sense of integrity. The cultural actor, like the madman, feels that he has no choice but to pursue these ends, and feels that his life cannot begin until he has grasped them. Like the patient, the self in culture is ambivalent about the mode of being in which he has immersed himself. The self in culture continually vacillates between, on the one hand, a sense of absurdity combined with a desire to be itself, and, on the other, a fearfulness that it cannot survive without being defined and owned by the collective. It thus perceives the bogus quality of the group reality but shrinks from full recognition. It turns its existence largely into an experience of living death, a suspension in time. Often when we stand "outside" a particular culture, we can perceive in totality what the members only suspect: that the social construction of reality can be quite mad.

In order to explore and illustrate this premise as a tool for the analysis of life in culture, we have chosen several small and relatively isolated groups for scrutiny. By dealing with their myths, beliefs, customs, and ritual practices, we may generate a clearer understanding of their organizing assumptions. We will emphasize several major themes, which recur with regularity across groups when they appear and seem to have emotional salience. The content of this material centers on a finite number of human concerns and representations of human intentions: nurturance, deprivation, enslavement, sexuality, aggression, fear, and vengeance. Once again, it is the structure of these concerns and intentions as they are seen, denied, distorted and enacted which is significant. Each theme is a symbol or locus for expressing feelings about one's relation to the self and reality.

Although the combinations of these themes can vary considerably, the scripts and plots they form tend to unfold along similar lines. That is, the self or protagonist suffers a sense of needful longing. He craves some object or attribute outside of himself to end his sense of inner deprivation, but is blocked in his quest. The world seems to stand in opposition to the self, forcing it into the heroic stance of aggressive striving or conquest. In this striving, the self feels morally justified. He is portrayed as contending against malevolent forces and fighting, it seems, for his own survival. These forces which threaten him are usually personified in the figure of the "monster" or "ogre." Such a metaphor carries with it a number of implications. The self need not feel guilt in slaying the monster. It may appear in humanoid form, but the monster is never entitled to be treated as fully human. Moreover, since the monster starts out with an inherent advantage over a mere mortal, the self must be transformed if it is to prevail. Ritual consistently enacts this transformation of the self into an object equivalent in mystery and power to the metaphoric ogre.

Finally, we must note the ambivalent, absurd quality of these "transformations" and the monstrous representations which provoke them. The members of these cultures continue to question the reality and efficacy of the ritual changes. There is a pervasive sense of doubt that the ritual is any more than a sham, that one is really safer because of what culture has given him. We even see intimations that these people doubt the existence and fearfulness of the mythic monsters. They do not discount these elements of their culture, but live as true believers while maintaining their doubts. The sense of estrangement from culture, or an appreciation of its absurdity, is not a "modern" aberration. It is endemic to all known groups. *This sense of estrangement is linked to the perception that culture represents the enactment of a myth or dream*— a mythic modality that is a response to the terror of living as one's self, the terror of what lurks within the depths of the self. The terror has its counterpart in a belief that others are malevolent, that monsters lurk "out there."

We begin by following Claude Lévi-Strauss's lead and cite one of the many myths told by the Borroro Indians of Central Brazil (2:35). As he shows, the myth is integral to the cultural weave of the entire area and shares key elements with numerous other myths. The following summary is drawn from his discussion in *The Raw and the Cooked* (2:35-38).

The legend, "the macaws and their nest," refers to the

"olden times" when the women of the tribe journeyed into the forest "to gather the palms used in the making of *ba*" (penis sheaths). The ba was presented to the youth of the tribe at the initiation ceremony, and was from then on a standard part of their dress. In the myth, one pre-initiate followed his mother into the forest, "caught her unawares, and raped her."

When the woman returned from the forest, her husband noticed feathers caught in her bark-cloth belt, which were similar to those worn by youths as an adornment. Suspecting that something untoward had occurred, he decreed that a dance should take place in order to find out which youth was wearing a similar adornment. But to his amazement he discovered that his son was the only one. The man ordered another dance, with the same result.

Convinced now of his misfortune and anxious to avenge himself, he sent his son to the "nest" of souls, with instructions to bring back the great dance rattle (bapo), which he coveted. The young man consulted his grandmother who revealed to him the mortal danger that such an undertaking involved; she advised him to obtain the help of the hummingbird.

When the hero, accompanied by the hummingbird, reached the aquatic region of souls, he waited on the shore, while the hummingbird deftly stole the rattle by cutting the short cord from which it was hanging. The instrument fell into the water, making a loud noise—jo. Alerted by this noise, the souls fired arrows from their bows. But the hummingbird flew so fast that he reached the shore safe and sound with the stolen rattle.

The father then ordered his son to fetch the small rattle belonging to the souls; and the same episode was repeated, with the same details, only this time the helpful animal was the quick flying juriti [a kind of dove]. During a third expedition, the young man stole some buttore; these are jingling bells made from the hoofs of . . . a wild pig, which are strung on a piece of rope and worn as anklets. He was helped by the large grasshopper . . . which flew more slowly than the birds so that the arrows pierced it several times but did not kill it.

Furious at the foiling of his plans, the father invited his son to come with him to capture the macaws, which were nesting in the face of a cliff. The grandmother did not know how to ward off this fresh danger, but gave her grandson a magic wand to which he could cling if he happened to fall.

The two men arrived at the foot of the rock; the father erected a long pole and ordered his son to climb it. The latter had hardly reached the nests when the father knocked the pole down; the boy only just had time to thrust the wand into a crevice. He remained suspended in the void, crying for help, while the father went off.

Our hero noticed a creeper within reach of his hand; he grasped hold of it and with difficulty dragged himself to the top of the rock. After a rest he set out to look for food, made a bow and arrows out of branches, and hunted the lizards which abounded on the plateau. He killed a lot of them and hooked the surplus ones to his belt and to the strips of cotton wound round his legs and ankles. But the dead lizards went bad and gave off such a vile smell that the hero fainted. The vultures . . . fell upon him, devoured first of all the lizards, and then attacked the body of the unfortunate youth, beginning with his buttocks. Pain restored him to consciousness, and the hero drove off his attackers which, however, had completely gnawed away his hindquarters. Having eaten their fill, the birds were prepared to save his life; taking hold of his belt and the strips of cotton round his arms and legs with their beaks, they lifted him into the air and deposited him gently at the foot of the mountain.

The hero regained consciousness "as if he were awaking from a dream." He was hungry and ate wild fruits but noticed that since he had no rectum, he was unable to retain his food, which passed through without even being digested. The youth was at first nonplussed and then remembered a tale told him by his grandmother, in which the hero solved the same problem by molding for himself an artifical behind out of dough made from pounded tubers.

After making his body whole again by this means and eating his fill, he returned to his village, only to find that it had been abandoned. He wandered around for a long time looking for his family. One day he spotted foot and stick marks, which he recognized as being those of his grandmother. He followed the tracks but, being anxious not to reveal his presence, he took on the appearance of a lizard, whose antics fascinated the old woman and her other grandson, the hero's younger brother. Finally, after a long interval, he decided to reveal himself to them. In order to re-establish contact with his grandmother, the hero went through a series of transformations, turning himself into four birds and a butterfly, all unidentified . . .

On that particular night there was a violent wind accompanied by a thunder storm which put out all the fires in the village except the grandmother's. Next morning everybody came and asked her for hot embers, in particular the second wife of the father who had tried to kill his son. She recognized her stepson, who was supposed to be dead, and ran to warn her husband. As if there were nothing wrong, the latter picked up his ceremonial rattle and welcomed his son with the songs of greeting for returned travelers.

However, the hero was full of thoughts of revenge. One day while he was walking in the forest with his little brother, he broke off a branch of the api tree, which was shaped like a deer's antler. The child, acting on his elder brother's instructions, then managed to make the father promise to order a collective hunt; in the guise of a mea, a small rodent, he secretly kept watch to discover where their father was lying in wait for the game. The hero then donned the false antlers, changed into a deer, and rushed at his father with such ferocity that he impaled him on the horns. Without stopping, he galloped toward a lake, into which he dropped his victim,

*who was immediately devoured by the Buiogoe spirits who
are carnivorous fish. All that remained after the gruesome
feast were the bare bones which lay on the bottom of the
lake, and the lungs which floated on the surface in the form
of aquatic plants, whose leaves, it is said, resemble lungs.*

*When he returned to the village, the hero took his revenge
on his father's wives (one of whom was his own mother).*
(2:35–38)

The Borroro myth lays out the elements of what will become a familiar drama. Women attempt to capture or own
the penises of young men through magic or ritual means.
They provide them with a penis sheath, which is a replacement or social penis for the adult male. Women provide the
erect, visible penis, enclosing or hiding the original penis. The
boy rapes, or wishes to rape, his mother. He attempts to do
this prior to initiation and prior to having his penis tampered
with. The father, who cannot let this "wrong" pass unpunish-
ed, feels compelled to destroy and/or castrate his son for his
crime, but seems reluctant to carry out the execution and provides the son chances to circumvent punishment. The father
acts only indirectly as the agent of punishment. He launches
the son on a perilous journey, the objective of which is theft.
Moreover, the victims of the proposed theft are to be the
tribal ancestors or souls (having committed one crime against
his progenitors, the hero is asked to commit another in the
name of filial devotion). On one level, this last is a paternal
ruse for leading the boy to destruction. On a second level, the
act appears more equivocal, putting the son in peril but also
giving him opportunity to prevail.

Another ambivalent element enters in that the grandmother
(or mother surrogate) allies herself with the boy, and provides the methods of his escape. This is obviously a curious
state of affairs. The helping grandmother must either be the
mother of the incestuously raped woman or the mother of
her aggrieved husband. It is also curious that the raped

mother herself raises no complaint and does not identity her assailant. The "crime" calls for vengeance but the mother exhibits a singular lack of concern over her violation. The cuckolded father begins by refusing to believe in the guilt of his son, and trying to produce other suspects (calls for a second dance). Even when the identity of the wrongdoer becomes obvious, the father neither punishes nor admonishes him, but pushes him into perilous situations. Instead of acting against the son, the father seems to be testing him through a series of ordeals: the father ultimately acted "as if there were nothing wrong . . . and welcomed his son with the songs of greeting for returned travelers." Grandmother and brother show no rancor toward the protagonist for his deed, and there is no mention of any group condemnation of his act.

In this myth the rape of a mother is not regarded as an abomination. The listener identifies with the perpetrator, not those who would punish him. The rape itself is not a consummation but the beginning of an odyssey. The adventures revolve around a few motifs: theft, castration (snipping off hanging rattles, chopping down poles, having one's buttocks eaten away), penetration (being shot by arrows, birds eating into one's bowels, spearing with antlers), struggling against obliteration, being in a kind of dream, wandering. A strong element of the drama is transformation, both of parts of the self and the whole. One castrated member—the buttocks—must be replaced artificially in the course of this wandering. The protagonist does not return to the tribe as himself, but rather as "a lizard, four birds and a butterfly" (2:30).

The adolescent does not simply mature into manhood through some natural process, for it is not the original hero who returns to the tribe. To achieve adulthood, the very nature of the hero's self must be altered. The myth provides a number of associations to the lizard form: they are food, "vile," they hang from the hero's belt, they attract castrating vultures. This raises the suspicion that the lizard is the symbolic equivalent of the penis and also that it is regarded ambivalently. There are countertendencies for the lizard to be good and bad, valuable and harmful. They cause the hero to lose body parts (be castrated) but also to be saved and, indeed, be saved by the castrators themselves (the vultures). This sequence reinforces the association between penis and lizard. It is the "vile" activity of the penis (mother rape) which first leads to the hero's jeopardy (i.e., first attracts the attention of the castrating father). The vultures, like the father, are ambivalent. They begin the process of destroying the hero, but save him instead.

It may also be significant that the vultures save him only after he is no longer "himself," but has been forced to fashion new body parts. The rule of the initiation ceremony is finally obeyed. The protagonist cannot survive as a man without an artificial penis (ba). Moreover, the use of an artificial member enhances his apparent potency in several ways. Donning "false antlers" allows the protagonist to "impale" the father and have him eaten by "carnivorous fish." The boy is no longer simply a rapist, but also a murderer. If mutilation was the penalty for rape, patricide now becomes the precondition for it. The boy rapes and is punished; the man kills and takes what he wants. In killing, the boy assumes the father's prerogatives. The symbol of the father's death is that of cannibalistic devouring—the "gruesome feast."

The hero has become strong enough to replace his father through alliance and theft, not through growth or virtue. The destruction of the patriarch is made possible by the formation of fraternity. The younger brother becomes allied with the hero. He tricks the father into a position of vulnerability, is himself transformed into another order of being (a small rodent), and acts as a spy for the hero.

The qualities and objects that enhance both hero and younger brother are extrinsic. They are borrowed, found, recruited, or stolen. One is forced into the world to give up the self, to become a new self and to get the strength to act from objects "out there." The self, acting alone, would perish. The grandmother, hummingbird, grasshopper, magic wand, lizards, buzzards, pounded tubers, brother, deer's antlers, and carnivorous fish are all crucial in keeping the hero alive. One could interpret this as a metaphor that cooperation and the use of objects in the natural environment are useful to survival. On the other hand, the movement of the story militates against such a straightforward interpretation. The "natural" objects are used in a struggle between humans (father and son) over social prerogatives, and in the mission of theft from ancestors. They are used in fantastic ways and are valued for qualities other than the utilitarian: the hummingbird for its speed, the vultures for their flight, the deer for its antlers. The hero does not use the creatures, he borrows qualities from them to become more than human. There is a blurring of boundaries between the hero and the objects he uses. They do his bidding, become virtual extensions of him. His intentions sometimes seem to emanate from the creatures (fish eat father). The hero, at the same time, becomes the animals he is using. We become confused as to his essential nature as he takes on new parts and transforms himself into nonhuman species.

There is further blurring of boundaries in the alliances that develop. What might be a very personal fight between the hero and his father becomes a group affair. We are not told why the younger brother allies with the hero against father, but the ensuing patricide is clearly a joint endeavor. The vengeance the hero is seeking has become diluted, less personal.

Finally, there is a balance to the saga. The myth ends as it begins: "the hero took his revenge on his father's wives (one of whom was his mother)" (2:31). However, the transformations undergone in the odyssey have altered the situation. The avenging hero at the end need not fear retribution. The vulnerable boy raped with his own member. He survives the challenge of castration in the process of wandering, and takes the artificial member. He returns as something other than himself. This new agent can rape with impunity. He is allowed to possess women; he is a man.

The assumptions and fears—the meaning—underlying this myth can be unraveled only by reference to the surrounding context. Although the dramatic action centers on mother rape and the subsequent struggle with the father, the allusions in the myth tie the hero's odyssey to major institutions, beliefs, and practices in the culture. One obvious parallel is with the ordeal of initiation. Indeed, as Lévi-Strauss points out, the myth begins with a reference to initiation rites. Many of the elements have analogs in the prescribed ritual. The actual initiation lasted between "several months" and a "whole year," its limit being signaled by a death occurring in the village. This was done so that the final ceremonial could coincide with the funeral rites. Observers agree that the initiation journey represented a grueling experience. Often several hundred miles in length, this "wandering" of the young man was directed by the adult males, who did not attempt to minimize the suffering of the initiates.

The ritual is described as follows:

> When they were finally brought back, hirsute, emaciated and completely covered with leaves, their respective mothers had to identify them before taking them off to wash and shave them and do their hair. The novices performed ritual leaps over a fire, and the ceremony of the return ended with everyone bathed in the river.

> Mothers greeted their sons by "weeping bitterly and uttering cries and lamentations as if for the death of some loved one." They wept because, from now on, the boy, having been emancipated, would leave the woman to go to live with the men. Also from now on until the end of his life, the young men would wear the *ba*, or penis sheath. (2:43-44)

This final aspect of the ceremony gains significance because "[o]nly after he has been fitted with the *ba* was the young man allowed to marry" (2:45). A male figure is interposed between novice and bride even at this point. The women gather the material and manufacture the *ba*, but it is the men who must put it in place. More specifically, a sponsor is chosen to manage the fitting of the sheath. This sponsor must be drawn from the opposite *moiety* (tribal subdivision) than that of the novice. He is also a member of one of the specific subclans from which the youth can take a bride. The initiation ceremony ends with "the novice offer[ing] food to his sponsor, observing the same ritual conventions as would a wife with her husband" (2:45). One investigator thus "concluded that in the minds of the indians it would seem that the jorrubbadare (sponsor) represented the future wife" (2:46). The initiated "marries" the male sponsor as a precondition to taking a woman. The matter does not end here. Lévi-Strauss, citing new information in the *Enciclopedia Bororo*, indicates that the

> sexual symbolism of the ba is [even] more complex. According to the new account, the novice's grandfathers and elder brothers first of all take a bud . . . from the babassu plant and offer it to the man whom they have chosen to play the part of sponsor, saying to him: "This (bud) will in truth be your bride." The sponsor then [makes] the leaves into penis sheaths, which the novice wears around his head all night, strung together in the form of a crown. Next morning the sponsor is led back to the novice who is still wearing his crown, and the formula is repeated. Thereupon one sheath is picked out, and the novice . . . holds it between his teeth . . ,

> If the theory that "the young babassu shoot and the penis sheath . . . represent the female organ, since they are called the sponsor's brides" were confirmed, it would completely alter our ideas about the symbolism of the penis sheath . . .

not with the feminine sex in general, but with the women
of the moiety and even of the clan and subclan to which
the novice belongs and with which the sponsor's subclan
prefers to intermarry—in other words, with those women
who might be the sponsor's "brides" and who . . . play an
active part in the gathering of the palms, a detail that
suggests the same identification figuratively. (2:46)

The web of symbolism becomes increasingly convoluted.
There is some confusion over who is to take a bride: sponsor,
novice, or both. The symbolic bride is represented as a gift of
the "novice's grandfathers and elder brothers." Penis sheaths
are worn as a crown: the total body is equated with the penis.
The novice must hold the sheath in his teeth prior to fitting,
suggesting self-fellatio. Although the marriage custom demands exogamy, the sheath which the penis enters is said to
symbolize "the female organ [of] the woman of the moiety
and even of the clan and subclan to which the novice belongs . . ." (2:46)

The plot is now familiar, but expanded. The ritual of initiation is largely an enactment of the key myth. The young
man, seeking sexual access, undergoes a series of ordeals. In
the actual initiation ceremony the trials are established by the
male seniors (father surrogates). Like the mythic hero, the
initiate becomes a wanderer. He is thus transformed into
something "hirsute, emaciated and covered with leaves," perhaps reminiscent of the lizard of the myth. In the ritual it is
the mother herself who identifies her son, bringing him back
to a human shape. This lends further credence to the notion
that the grandmother in the myth is in fact a mother surrogate, or part of a fractionated maternal image. A prerequisite
to this terminal phase of the ritual is a death in the village,
just as the murder of the father must precede the son's manhood in the myth. This motif is reinforced by the maternal at-
titude of weeping bitterly and uttering cries and lamentations
as if for the death of some loved one" (2:44). The death

of the father is, in a sense, a double death. The women, we are told, mourn because "until the end of his life, the young man would wear the ba, or penis sheath" (2:44). The "loved one" who dies is, obviously, the natural son. The transformation of boy into man is also a death or murder. The ba is purchased by the loss of one's own penis, which, as we have seen, is equated with the total self at a later point in the ritual. The youth is transformed from an agent who potentially uses his own penis to take what he wants (mother), to a more passive object, taking what he is given by his elders (the gift-bride). The heterosexual crime of the pre-initiate is replaced by the homosexually tinged legal possession of the initiate. In order to mate, he must first submit to the men, and "marry" a man, acting out the role of wife. Even at this point in the ritual, we see the same motivation that underlies the hero's action in the myth. Although marriage must be exogamous, the entrance of the penis into the sheath represents incest. The sheath is equated with the vagina of taboo women.

In both the myth and the ritual the peril of living as one's self is circumvented by "death" and transformation. One gives up being one's self (dies), in order to continue existing. Natural sex with a self-chosen other is replaced by normatively legitimate sex with an object chosen by one's elders. The initiate must part from his mother and join the homosexual fraternity of men. His subsequent approach to women is always as a member of this group, and under its rules. Ambivalence still remains. The mythic hero is the pre-initiate outlaw; to be fitted with the penis sheath is not only to submit but also to enter the taboo woman (mother).

The Borroro myth and initiation rite are revealing of a number of shared wishes and equations. Moreover, they bear striking similarity to elements found in markedly divergent cultures. Bettelheim quotes Malinowski on initiation rites as follows:

They present right through the vast range of their occurrence certain striking similarities. Thus the novices have to undergo a more or less protracted period of seclusion and preparation. Then comes initiation proper, in which the youth, passing through a series of ordeals, is finally submitted to an act of bodily mutilation: at the mildest a slight incision or the knocking out of a tooth; or, more severe, circumcision; or, really cruel and dangerous, an operation such as the subincision [in initiation, the young man's penis is slit from base to glans with a stone knife] practiced in some Australian tribes. The ordeal is usually associated with the idea of the death and rebirth of the initiated one, which is sometimes enacted in a mimetic performance. (1:18)

Bettelheim, cataloging a number of initiation ceremonies and explanatory myths, suggests that fear and envy of women is one strong element dramatized in these elaborate enactments. He cites the ritual song of a central Australian tribe, which saga connects the rites of circumcision and subincision with the two mythical Wawilak sisters. In the mythology of the region they are the first human beings to walk the earth, the mothers of the species to whom tribal members see a direct lineage. The initiation rite is a reenactment of these origin myths, wherein men cut their penises or arms off to create bleeding and vulva-like openings, thus becoming symbolically able to menstruate and bear children. An accompanying song indicates that the women demand that circumcision take place.

If we listen to the participants, it would appear that men mutilate (and perhaps castrate) themselves and one another, not because of fear of a dominating male figure, but because of the largely fantasized threat posed by women or female imagos. Bettelheim describes the evolution of initiation rites at puberty among a group of schizophrenic children, patients in his residential institution. The first menses among the girls in the group appeared to trigger the interactions that led to the establishment of a phenomenologically similar ritual. He observes that the adolescent girls appear to "recoil" openly from menstruation. At the same time, they attribute magical power to the process, and "it holds an irresistible fascination for them" (1:27). The girls seem to revel in the power it provides them, particularly the power to "make boys uncomfortable if not plainly anxious" (1:27). This force seems magical to the females because they need do nothing to obtain or exercise it. It is theirs simply because they are female: it is a mystery over which they have no control. These very qualities make femaleness frightening and dangerous. Feeling one's self to be the receptacle for a destructive force can be unsettling. Bettelheim observes of his patients that "the girl who experiences her menses this way has not really accepted or emotionally mastered the function, but remains partly at its mercy. She is not in control of her "sorcery," but at best a sorcerer's apprentice" who at any moment may find herself subject to her own witchcraft" (1:27). Women have secret, magical functions that both attract boys and frighten them. Women are torn between the tendency to hide or disown the "proof" of these powers and the wish to flaunt them. Menstruation is what makes the girl powerful and valuable, gives her a locus of self. It is also dirty, profane, and dangerous. The female processes demand that the girl have the strength to utilize or subdue her inherent powers. They also invoke in the girl the fear of being overwhelmed or out of control. She both relishes and resents the onset of her menses. Bettelheim provides some information on the symbolic or experiential processes through which this state of affairs connects to the male initiation rite. He observes that negative feelings toward the female functions lead readily to hostility toward boys, and especially toward the penis. They feel that, in order to redress the balance, boys should also bleed from their genitals. Bettelheim goes on to illustrate that when the girl cannot induce the boys to engage in such bloody ritual, she may designate

some part of her body as a penis, which she can herself mutilate.

> One twelve year old schizophrenic girl felt most of the time
> that she despised her femininity and wished she were a boy.
> But at other times she believed herself to be both boy and
> girl . . . At such times she often acted out intercourse
> symbolically, using her index finger as an erect penis and a
> circular object for the vagina. But it was not her index
> finger in its normal condition that became her penis; it
> was the finger only in erect stiffness, This she called "my
> fingerbone" and differentiated it clearly from her finger as
> such. Whenever she had a fingerbone, it was a penis, and
> she was unable (or unwilling) to bend it at its joints. When
> she used the finger for other (even sexual) purposes, as
> when masturbating, it was just a finger, easily bent.

> For many months, whenever she menstruated, she wanted
> to cut this fingerbone to make it bleed. (1:28)

If one sees why women might wish to subject men to this
ordeal, it is less easy to comprehend why the men go along.
On the one hand, Bettelheim remarks that "it was the girls,
not the boys who inaugurated the plans; and it was the boys'
fear of their overpowering mothers (not fathers) that seemed
important in making them accept the girls' proposals" (1:43).
On the other hand, he cites instances, in Chicago and in
Cuba, where adolescent boys put each other through ordeals
or trials, as well as inflicting pain on the male organ, as a
prerequisite to joining the all-male gang (1:34). If women
play any part in these rituals, it is typically as objects of conquest by which the boy demonstrates his masculinity. The
boys, it would seem, wish to do that which the girls demand
of them. The schizophrenic boys, for example, exhibited
"their willingness to suffer pain in order to assure entrance to
an adult society which, they imagined, freely enjoyed sex . . .

pain in initiation is the price adolescents pay for the prerogatives of adulthood" (1:43). What is highly striking here is
that no one is demanding this price from them, yet they feel
constrained to pay it. The girls are no objective threat to
them; there are no cultural elders enforcing ritual dictum.
This spontaneous initiation arises as an antidote to the actors'
fears, and is experienced as a means of self-transformation.
To the observer, these contingencies and terrors are no more
nor less than fantasies. The actors, however, seem to find
them frightening and compelling and do not pause to consider
their substantiality.

What objective, fantasized or real, are men trying to achieve
in these rites? The origins of male ceremonial are tied to envy
and to theft. The men clearly regard women as having a secret.
It is related to the female physiology, procreative function,
and associated mystery. Nor are women's secrets counterbal-
anced by male mysteries. Women, in fact, can be openly
derisive at the very idea of men's secrets. If we return to the
Central Australian origin myths, they make it manifest that
the men originally "had nothing: no sacred objects, no sacred
ceremonies, the women had everything" (1:123). Unable to
tolerate this state of affairs, the men raided the women's camp,
stealing their sacred objects. The Wawilak sisters seem to dis-
miss this act as a juvenile prank of no consequence. Indeed,
they thought it "just as well" that the men had "stolen" the
secrets.

Or as one of Berndt's present-day informants told him:
"But really we have been stealing what belongs to them
(the women), for it is mostly all woman's business; and
since it concerns them it belongs to them. Men have nothing
to do really, except copulate, it belongs to the women. All
that belonging to those *Wawilak*, the baby, the blood, the
yelling; their dancing, all that concerns the women; but
every time we have to trick them. Women can't see what
men are doing, although it really is their own business, but

we can see their side . . . in the beginning we had nothing, because men had been doing nothing; we took these things from the women." (1:123)

The men wish to become as good (useful) as women, as powerful and as mysterious. In this they are only partly successful, since they remain as children playing games, while the women appear as disdainful or amused mothers. The men are permitted to act out the fantasy of power, for the women feel that this power will remain their own for all time. The fantastic lengths to which men collectively go to perpetuate their bogus claims is well documented. The connection between the male ruse and menstruation is manifest.

Blackwood, for example, has referred to the secrecy surrounding the boys' wearing of the *upi*, a tall, awkward and probably uncomfortable hat made of palm leaves, which conceals the hair. The *upi* is put on while the boy's hair is short, and he wears it until initiation, never taking it off in the presence of women until it is ceremonially removed. On its removal, the women suddenly discover the mysterious secret of men: they have long hair. The main purpose of the ceremony is to surprise the women with the length of the hair.

The Buka have three initiation ceremonies, the first of which is the donning of the *upi*, and the second its removal. In girls, the growing of the breasts may precede menstruation by some time; likewise the boys put on the *upi*, in the seclusion of the bush at about the age of nine, and take it off several years later. The terms used to designate pubertal boys and girls emphasize this parallel. The girl is called "a female whose breasts are developing." while of the boy they say, "he goes to the bush," meaning he has withdrawn to put on the *upi*.

Since so little actually happens—in this instance, such an ordinary phenomenon as the hair's growth—it is particularly necessary to declare it a great secret and to ritualize it. Only in this way can they pretend that what happens to boys at puberty is as important as what happens to girls. The *upi,* ridiculous though it may look to the foreign observer, is probably the most serious and important factor in the whole culture of this area. Its rules and taboos profoundly influence the people's daily life. (1:126)

Another example both reinforces this point and sheds further light on the meaning of the "hoax."

The Chaga men, in a society where the importance attached to menstrual blood is very great, claim ascendancy over women by acquiring power over a bodily function that women cannot control. They maintain that during initiation the anus is stopped up permanently and that after that men retain their feces. To be "stopped up" is identical with acquiring the rights of an adult male. This stopping up of the anus is the central rite of initiation; the novices are told that the plug is the sign of manhood and that guarding its secret is their first duty. Thus:

"Don't emit wind in the presence of women and uninitiated youth. If you do, the tribal elders will slaughter your cows. Neither must you be surprised by women when you defecate. Always carry a stick with you, dig your feces in, and scratch about here and there pretending that you are digging for some charm. Then if a woman should observe you, she will seek there and find nothing. . . . If you suffer from looseness of the bowels, call on one of your age mates to take you to the men's house to look after you there, for if your bride gets to know about it, it means misery to you. If you dare to tell anybody of the secret of men, then your age group, the tribal elders and the chief will without mercy deprive you of all you own. For you will have disgraced your contemporaries, yea the very dead themselves. And it will be said that the secret of the men is a lie.' The novices were therefore trained openly in basing their manhood on a fiction." (1:128)

A remarkable feature of this fiction is that no one believes it. If its ostensible purpose is to fool and intimidate women, it seems to serve opposite ends. The women not only see through the "mystery," but analyze its origin. In the end it only makes them feel increasingly superior to the men, whom they indulge in their nonsense:

> The Chaga women, who are aware of what is going on, regard the men's behavior with amused tolerance. In their own initiation rites, the girls are told that the men defecate but keep it secret from the women, and they are admonished not to laugh. The women realize that actually the secret is theirs; they say that when a woman becomes pregnant her source of blood is stopped up and that this is the original plug.

The women's inference that men want to become something they are not is corroborated by other features of the ritual. It is not simply that the men wish to have a "secret" of their own. They act to create a secret which is the exact analog of the bleeding and childbearing of women. Both Bettelheim and Roheim comment on the fact that the "setting of the plug" is highly reminiscent of the manner in which the Chaga deal with menstruation (3:120; 1:128-29). The men are taught to hide their feces in precisely the manner in which the women hide the menstural blood and for a parallel reason: to hide these taboo products from the opposite sex. "Roheim recognized that the secrecy surrounding the male rites seemed like a simple inversion of the menstruation taboo, the men saying 'We are not allowed to see your bleeding so we shall not allow you to see ours' " (1:129).

The Chaga men apparently want to go beyond creating an antidote to women's power. They indeed want to become as women, to gain the ultimate power of giving birth to themselves:

> To this end, they exclude women entirely from the initiation ceremony, which is represented as a new birth. These features of the ritual can be seen as expressions of the need to assert the co-equality of the male role, and of rights over their progeny. This they try to achieve by demonstration that the care they have exercised to arouse fecundity and to make it secure, equals the accomplishment of the mother on the occasion of giving birth to a child . . .

> The presence of setting the *ngoso* [plug], for example, is justified by the Chaga because it was necessary in order to create and secure respect of the women [for the men].

> . . . If the content of the initiation ceremonies is a reshaping of men so that they can procreate, and if this reshaping is experienced primarily as a rebirth, then it is suggestive to set in parallel the time of men's preparation for procreation with the time period which the infant spends in the mother's womb, namely nine months. The period of caretaking after circumcision lasts for two or three months. The stay in the [initiation] grove where the teaching takes place lasts six months. In this way nine months elapse from the beginning of the ceremonies until their end, the final setting of the plug. Undoubtedly the most important mark of pregnancy aroused their interest. Through it they designate pregnancy and say: *mak akufungje*: the woman closes herself up. The setting of the *ngoso* probably, therefore, originally was to represent the counterpart to this on the part of the men. Moreover, it should surpass the contribution of women so that even greater honors were given to men. (1:129-30)

Through initiation men are born a second time. In this rebirth they are the sons of the fraternity of men. They are transformed from natural men into hermaphrodites, able to bear children. Paradoxically, they are socially defined as men only when they have subsumed the female functions. In this process the natural man dies, but it is only the mother who openly mourns. The key elements of the reborn man's self are stolen. He becomes worthy and viable by taking that which belongs to women.

The transformation remains, phenomenologically, a lie. Even the participants are unable to believe in it. The incredible means the men use to reassure themselves ultimately prove ineffective. "Because men began to doubt that circumcision and subincision had given them the desired magic power, they may have added new rites and ceremonies, hoping that these would provide it. But when their redoubled efforts still ended in failure, women's power may have seemed still more awesome and mysterious . . . Among some tribes the rituals finally become so intricate that the complete performance required years" (1:131).

We must emphasize again that these rituals and myths are not isolated or peripheral parts of the cultures described. They are central to the whole structure of social roles, beliefs, and tribal rules which govern the daily lives of the participants. The enactments described often consume more time and energy than actual survival behaviors. They are clearly treated just as seriously by the participants as, say, food gathering. Moreover, the inventiveness and technology manifest in the creation and enactment of these metaphors equals or exceeds the amount of thoughtfulness given to "practical" issues. It is in the creation of the ritual artifacts that these peoples exhibit their greatest skill and artfulness. Their myths are not misconstruals of reality, they are the reality that the self lives out while never quite believing in it.

We have attempted to show the general identity between culture and myth; we have also sought to illustrate how ritual represents an enactment of collective myth. Although we have concentrated on "primitive" cultures, we do not see them as fundamentally different from advanced cultures in this respect. Both are built on the mythic modality. Ritual is the mechanism through which culture becomes a representation of myth. These allegorical productions represent an attempt to portray an inner experience of fear, longing, and ambivalence.

The language by which the self and the collective express these inner processes is that of metaphor. The metaphor is the building block of the myth: the spear is the metaphor of the erect, avenging penis; the mythic Wawilak sisters are the metaphoric representation of female nurturance, primacy, and mystery. One feature of the metaphors—and the myths which are derived from them—is that they are overcondensed and distorted. That is, cultural members push their meaning and use to extreme limits, often going beyond their experiential base. Although men may wish for penises as rigid, long, and frightening as a spear, and may even glory in their erections, the wish does not change the reality. Women may sometimes seem to be the origin of life, but the Wawilak sisters did not by themselves create man, and the tribal members are well aware of this fact.

The self attempts to use these fundamental metaphors to control and clarify its own disquietude. In this process it comes to realize the essential inaccuracy of the collective metaphor in conveying experiences. In this realization lies the basis for the nagging sense of unreality associated with myth and ritual. The self wishes that the metaphor were a perfect encapsulation of its feelings and longings. As such the metaphor is seen as the device that can free one from himself. The self attempts to enter the cultural myth as if it would release one from fear or a sense of incompleteness. But myth and ritual do not serve this end, for inner disquietude remains a property of one's experience of being even if the self is faithful to ritual prescriptions. Each actor inevitably perceives this dilemma and feels defrauded. Nonetheless, he continues to cling to the myth as if his terror and longing would become totally overwhelming were he ever to let go. The original fears, we must note again, are fantasies of what lurks "out there." Once the self enters the metaphoric system of myth and ritual, "out there" becomes identified as the experiential territory not defined by these myths. The original fears that drive one to need culture as a way of defining reality may remain unabated. They have, however, been partially translated so as to leave one feeling a need for culture, even if there is no solace in clinging to it. The actor in culture becomes accustomed to the assumption that his suffering, no matter how profound, can only increase should he ever turn away from his culture.

By collectivizing myths into tribal rules, each man is helped to control this ambivalence which continually pushes him to question culture. If one is tempted to explore new ways of coming to grips with himself, the collective can help discourage action on this frightful possibility. To the extent that the self is enraged by the failure of ritual to transform his life, he finds in this same ritual safe outlets for expressing his anger. Men do not, then, believe in the worlds defined by their culture; they acquiesce to these definitions while continuing to experience their arbitrary, absurd quality.

References

1. Bruno Bettelheim, *Symbolic Wounds*, New York, Collier Books (1952).
2. Claude Lévi-Strauss, *The Raw and the Cooked: Introduction to a Science of Mythology*, Vol. 1, New York, Harper and Row (1964).
3. Geza Roheim, *The Eternal Ones of the Dream*, New York, International Universities Press (1969).
4. Philip E. Slater, *The Glory of Hera*, Boston, Beacon Press (1968).

6. Culture as Absurdity

Simultaneously perceiving oneself as alienated from culture and struggling to deny that self-perception can be an exquisitely complex task. Group myths and their ritual enactments establish a basic scenario for the mode of bad faith this task represents. The scenario is constructed of paradox, each element of myth and ritual containing its own negation. Moreover, the disbelief that opens the possibility of alienation is in fact built into the myth system. This aspect of culture represents a sort of releasing mechanism, permitting the self to stay in the dream while occasionally knowing it as such. The cultural recognition of the absurd helps the self to isolate and control his sense of alienation, to remain immersed in bad faith.

The recognition that myth and ritual are shared delusions has a self-mocking quality that is two-edged. It informs the self of the absurdity of its own position in becoming a cultural object rather than being himself. It also points to the basic absurdity of the collective dream, which is ultimately a pointless tale leading nowhere. The terms of this tale do, however, concretize for the self the vague longings, fears, and animosities that underlie bad faith. The cultural saga defines the monsters one must flee, the injustices the self must revenge, and the disguises he should adopt in living as something other than himself. The way in which the self is both attracted to and repelled by these paradoxes and prescriptions can be better understood by examining the specific forms they take in the cultures we have begun to look at.*

Let us try further to understand the Chaga ceremonial and the larger themes of which it is a part.

As Roheim repeatedly points out, even where myth and cultural explanation distort the function of the sexes in pro-creation (as with the Chaga), cultural members, in fact, know the "truth," in much the same terms as do Westerners (3, ch. 6). Myth continues to express the recognized (although de-nied) centrality of the female function. The rock or founda-tion of culture is the eternal mother, mother earth. It is she who is feared and yearned for, and who pervades all cultural images.

> This mother is always present behind the ritual, the dancing, and the singing. She is a symbol of the productive qualities of the earth, the eternal replenisher of human, animal, and natural resources; it was from her uterus that human and totemic beings came forth . . . she is the background of all totemic ceremony, an "eternal" explanation and symbol of the Aboriginal way of life, with its continual expectation of rebirth.

> The mother herself, *Kunapipi*, *Kalwadi*, or *Kadjari*, is represented in certain parts of the mythology as a perpetually pregnant woman, who in the Dream-Time let out from her uterus human beings, the progenitors of the present natives. She was responsible too for sending out spirits of the natural species from season to season, to ensure their continual increase. (1:170-71)

We see, then, the generation of myth and countermyth,

---

*The extended footnotes to this chapter, beginning on p. 200, are for readers who are interested in some further elaboration of the myths and rituals we cite and interpret in the text.

ritual and counter-ritual. Women are central; women are earth, culture, the origin, creation. Ritual and myth are not simply fabrication but also negation. Women are unnecessary; men can procreate, men dominate. Men become women. Men realize they can never become women. Men go through rituals to produce fear and respect in women. Women laugh at the men's efforts as pathetic, but participate in the ceremonial and do not reveal that they know the secret of the travesty. There is tremendous energy expended in the creation of a mammoth lie, its maintenance or protection, and finally its negation. The whole game has been treated with the greatest seriousness for countless generations, but everyone in the culture knows that it is nevertheless silly, amusing.

According to the game, he who is already born must die and be reborn. His rebirth is dependent on obtaining something which belongs to another, but the very thing he must steal (female mystery) is largely fantastic. That is, it is associated with physical phenomena but has been overlaid with fantastic meanings and received obsessive concern. Women are not so awesome in themselves. It is the metaphoric woman of myth who invokes dread. Women may bear children, but why need the men regard this ability as a fearful power? For some reason, men choose to feel incomplete and imperiled because they are not women. They correspondingly seek to assume an identity which protects them, but which is also impossible. The man lives as something bogus and as something which fails in its aim (protection from and equality with women). If anything, the senselessness has become even more inexplicable. We can note, however, that this male-female cleavage follows a general pattern—it is one of several basic antinomies that characterize culture. We will shortly explore the child-parent cleavage, which is but another representation of the same type of eternal warfare, but first let us pursue in greater depth the idea of eternal warfare between men and the fearful female imagos.

Recurrently, the only weapon the man can employ to prevail over a multitude of threatening demons is fire. By tribal
definitions and the origin myths of the Australians (similar to
our original Borroro tale), fire is the woman's possession. This
is clearly enacted in many of the Australian initiation ceremonies. Initiation is reported to climax in the following manner:
The assembled group waits until nightfall and then lights
many fires. The men and women establish separate camps on
opposite sides of the river. The fires in the women's camp are
discernible from the men's side, although partially shielded
by the forest. During the night the senior men shout across
the river and are answered by the women. The mood is of
"great excitement." One of the adult men calls out, inquiring
as to what the women are up to. A woman then replies, "We
are making a fire," and further threatens, "We are going to
burn the men." The men spend the night approaching and
running away from the fearful flames. Finally, they enter
the women's encampment. Each of the novices kneels before
a woman's fire while she stands behind him, pressing him
toward the smoke. It is only after thus engaging in symbolic
capitulation that the novice is able to move freely among the
women (1:162-63).

Women's power over fire and the men's corresponding fear
is further demonstrated in another initiation rite. In this Australian ceremony the men cover themselves with leaves and
small branches. Banding together into a tight group, they proceed toward the women's encampment. The initiates are sent
forward into the river bed, but behave in a hesitant manner.
They pause, approach the women, and then are set upon. The
women light flaming torches, throwing them "on the heads of
the men." The men attempt to use their own boughs for protection, but do not fight back. The older men encircle the
novices, moving around them while swinging the "bullroarer"
(a slab of wood with a hole cut in it). The men then turn
and run back toward the river, with the women in pursuit.
The women halt upon reaching the river, and return to their

own camp. After this phase of initiation, the men ostensibly feel "safe" with women, "who now ritually offer themselves as sex objects to the men" (1:164).

The process of conversion which takes place in initiation thus becomes more manifest. Women are dangerous. They own the flame, the power to consume. Men negate the women's power, either by capitulation as the price of immunity, or joint phallic action (see below), or both. Initiation manifests many elements of surrender. Boys must suffer, undergo ritual death, symbolic castration.

The initiate, as we shall see in more detail, symbolically surrenders his self, his claims to potency, in effect, saying to women, "you have no need to envy or desire me any longer." The men collectively perform the ritual of exposing their throats to the women's bared teeth. The women subjugate the men, but spare them. Such is the price of male survival.

In the series of dual hero myths, by which the Australians explain the origin of circumcision, "the boys all died"—that is, circumcision is a symbolic murder (4:68). The circumcision ceremony represents a modification and reduction of the original fantasied aggression. Mutilation is the price of survival. These origin myths further indicate that the male circumciser, using a knife, is an evolved form of the rite. The original tool of circumcision was the fire stick (or female weapon), and women were more active participants in the process. Even the surrender of maleness to the female monster does not remove anxiety; other means are sought to find "safety." The men seek to escape fearful women by becoming complete, coupling with themselves and claiming the power of procreation. Men begin by feeling vulnerable, join together into a homosexual gang, and become the aggressors. Men need one another for protection against women.

The precise threat that women pose is swallowing up male victims, orally or through the vagina in intercourse. Roheim reports that the "specific Central Australian anxiety in connection with coitus is that of penis captivus" (4:116). The men engage in aggressive joking about this, saying to one another, "If it takes too long you will be maimama (entrapped)." Women, it is feared, will grip the rim of the glans with the womb and refuse to release it.[1]

The concern with penis captivus is more than superficial. Sexual practices seem to indicate that it is taken seriously. "Before coitus, the women will stroke the penis downward toward the glans to excite the man, but the one thing a woman is never allowed to do is to catch hold of the glans penis" (4:116). In the sense that the rituals equate penis with the entire body and the self, the holding of the penis by the vagina, or "breaking it off," is tantamount to being consumed or giving up one's separateness.[2]

The men experience themselves as small boys, helpless in the face of the seductive onslaughts of the maternal or female imago. Men lust after women, but feel fearful and victimized. In the dream myth all desire resides in the overpowering woman. The ambivalent tenor of these fears will become more evident, but it is clear that men are fascinated by the terrifying situation. The problem of greed is also reversed in this aspect of the folklore. Men begin by coveting women's secrets, their essence. But maleness, through the symbol of the penis, now becomes elevated to a valued commodity. The Alknarintja women steals the penis, takes it into herself and refuses to relinquish it.[3] There is thus a mutuality of theft. Each sex wishes to rob and incorporate that which is exclusively the other's. Women, however, remain as the more fearful and powerful imagos.

An antidote to these fears is generated with relentless consistency in widely separated cultures. In the diverse settings under consideration, the stance of Heracles is the stance demanded in custom and ritual. Heracles embodies the prototypical defense, the male response to fear of the female imago. In Heracles' acts and statements we see a "compulsive assertion of strength" which is, at the same time, "a vigorous denial of weakness in the face of maternal hostility . . . he symbolizes exaggerated masculine differentiation . . . muscularity rather than virility *per se*" (5:339).

Men standing alone declare their inability to overcome a paralyzing fear of women, and turn to one another for strength. They experience their own selves as inadequate to the task of facing devouring females. In reaction to these feelings, the men either seek incorporation into a communal body with others, or take on artificial members to amplify their puny strength.

> Men seated around the campfire mutually masturbate each other and then compare whose penis is bigger. Curiously enough, however, the competition does not develop on the lines of who has the biggest one, but whose is the smallest. They say, "Mine is quite small, but yours is as big as a demon's (mamu)." Or they show the subincision openings to each other and say, "When you cohabit it grows so big that it bursts." The other retorts, "Yours is stiff as a bone," Counter retort: "Your penis is like a *muruntu* (dragon)." "Your subincision opening is like a *womera* (spear thrower)."

The men strive to have a penis that is adequate to the frightful task of coitus, or combat with women. On one level we can say that each feels an inner certainty that his own equipment is not up to the job. Each man wishes to buttress himself by alliance with others who are better off, who possess a more magnificent penis-weapon.

By joining the homosexual fraternity, the men endeavor to identify with a corporate penis, one less vulnerable than their own. Yet they cannot entirely get into this metaphor; they remain uncomfortable with the fiction they have created. Subincision is the precondition of fraternal membership—social manhood—but is also a source of shame. In the subincision, an essential part of initiation, the penis is slit from base to glans with a stone knife, after which the genitals must remain covered.[4]

The sequence becomes clear. Men are fearful and envious, attempt to transform themselves and must subsequently hide behind masks. This process makes them an embarrassment to themselves. They cannot present themselves as they are, but must fool the women. A woman cannot be subdued or attracted by the male, but only by the magic he can generate. "(I)n all primitive societies, falling in love and love magic are the same thing . . . (W)hen the boy whirls the bullroarer (tjuringa with hole punched in it) he sees his altjera (ancestor, double) penetrating into her own body and calling out her own name. This is how she falls in love with the boy" (4: 105). In this idea of love, we see the negation of female desire combined with the insulation or protection of the male. She desires not him but an apparition, his phallic double or ancestor. It is his double which penetrates or enters, leaving him remote or safe.

This self-elaboration, which is both depersonalization and penis aggrandizement, is carried to incredible lengths. The Inpirra tribe "sing" or bewitch the male's ornamentation that he might attract a woman. These incantations are performed on the shell which hangs over the penis and the feathers which form the young man's headdress. The male will touch his entire body with these now magical objects, making him irresistible to the woman he wishes to enchant. "The woman sees him with lightning crashing down to his right and left wherever he goes. She falls in love and runs to meet him." In the most powerful form of love magic, a "(ceremonial pole) is erected on the top of a hill. They go there several times and sing this pole. It develops into a *body* with the feathers as a head, and then becomes a man fully decorated for lovemaking. The women see lightning everywhere encircling him. They 'see this with the belly,' i.e., they feel it inside and the lightning draws them (*tjarinama*) towards the man" (3:84).

According to this formula men control or bring about female desire; women never choose a man as an object of lust, or make an approach. This is part of a larger cultural fiction, the concept of the Alknarintja or "eyes turn away" woman, who does not care for men (4:104). She is self-completing, self-gratifying, and "her resistance has to be broken down by force" (4:104). Women are defined as passive victims of the sexual act, which is instigated by the men. This definition ignores not only the thrust of much mythology, but also the behavioral reality available for all to observe—that is, women can and do act seductively in this culture.[5]

The men not only create fictions to ease their anxieties about being engulfed by female desire, but also utilize institutional means to protect themselves from the imagined threat posed by women. The most common method of obtaining a bride is through the *tualtja mara* arrangement, whereby men deal for the rights to the first daughters of women in their own age group. The contract, made before the child's birth, guarantees that the husband will be more than old enough to be the bride's biological father. Although everyone knows that the little girl has been promised to a certain man, "when the man comes to fetch her and grabs her arm she is frightened, breaks away and runs to her mother." Although based on contract, the transfer of child to betrothed is enacted with an element of abduction or force. As Roheim points out, "the essential thing is that the baby girl is handed over to a grown man" (4:103).[6] This can only be understood in the context of implacable fear of female magic, and in the joint assumption of sexual hostility combined with mutual need.

This is made apparent in the manner of approach to mature women which is conceived of and described in violent, adversary terms. Boys and girls "flirt" by attacking the totem belonging to the other.

> (T)he Aranda and the neighboring Loritja have a black bird as symbol of the men and a small pigeon as symbol of the women. The men will kill a pigeon and show it to the women, saying, "This belongs to you." . . . The men say when they have killed the bird that represents the woman,

"I have killed the thing that belongs to you." Among the Dieri both the men and the women have a plant as their "protector." When they wish to tease each other, the men root up the plant that belongs to the women and the women the men's plant.

If the young men seem to be rather slow in eloping with the available girls, the girls go out to the forest and with sticks kill some of the little birds called *jeerung*. They casually show the bird to the men; this results in an uproar. The men are angry, their brothers have been killed. The men and the girls both get sticks and beat each other till blood flows. Only the young men who are supposed to get married attend these fights. The newly initiated boys would avoid these scenes because they are afraid of seeing woman's blood. After a quarter of an hour the fighters are separated. Next day the young men go out and kill one of the women's "sisters," the bird *djeetgun*, and the consequence is an even worse fight. It takes a week or two till the wounds are healed. By and by, one of the marriageable young men meets one of the marriageable young women. He looks at her and says, "Djeetgun" (i.e., female totem). She laughs and says, "Yeerung" (male bird). "What does the yeerung eat?" the girl asks. The boy replies, "He eats so and so," mentioning some kind of game. They laugh and she runs off with him. (4:98-99)

Men and women are enemies; the coital act is one of aggression. In these tribes there is a single word for the first intercourse, marriage, and rape.[7] The coital position of the male is called "the spear thrower," and many rituals make this connection with equal explicitness. The penis is first and foremost a tool of aggression: coitus, ritual murder, or spearing. Myth once again shows how this belief is a reversal, a reaction to fear. The jeopardized penis, representing the self, becomes nonorganic and invulnerable.[8] The man must transform himself into a spear thrower in the name of self defense.

The transformation takes place in a context of both terror and greed. The man becomes a spear thrower so as to wrest from the world that which he feels is his.

There are numerous indications that the frightful and hated female which boys join together to slay is the mother. The male-female antinomy thus shares many representational elements with parent-child warfare. The little boy needs and covets his mother at the same time he fears and longs to kill her. In the Australian region under discussion, for example, the major protagonists in the myths are two wandering men. Normally portrayed as brothers, they are the fathers of the tribe. In one tale a mother gave birth to two baby boys. She filled a conch shell with milk and immediately abandoned her two offspring. The boys matured and underwent initiation, and then they set out to find their mother. Inquiring at each female group they encountered, they finally traced and apprehended her. They then slayed her with their spear. This, we are told, established "the tradition that very young children must be tended by their mother" (3:58).

The initial fraternal project is to spear the mother. Spearing is to make love, to rape, to marry, and to murder. To carry out this project, boys must become a fraternity and transform penises into spears. The fraternity seeks vengeance on the mother, and feels its mission to be just rather than brutal. The maternal sin is neglect; failure to provide endless gratification, failure to keep away the feelings of hunger and longing. The mother, on the other hand, feels justified in deserting or destroying her child on the same ground: self-defense. The child is represented in their demon lore as a voracious, insidious, little monster who will empty her of life if she is at all indulgent.[9] The infant seeks quiescence in the act of emptying the mother or re-entering her. The adults seem to find the infants an irresistible delicacy; children are thus in constant jeopardy of being devoured.

Certain aspects of the imagery employed (each man contains an infant; the infant is also a monster) may indicate that this division is essentially an internal one. The language of the metaphor shows that each actor experiences himself partially as imperiled, voracious infant and partially as powerful monster preying on helpless victims. These tales establish the image of a malevolent, paranoid world. One is always in danger of being obliterated by those with whom he is most intimate. Each actor lives in a state of longing and dread, feeling "compelled" to become murderous in order to satisfy a compulsive need.[10]

As if in reaction to this dreadful lust, the culture contains many practices that serve the function of protecting the infants.[11] For one group of tribes in this region, each member has two names, a "grandfather" name and an "ancestral" name. The former is bestowed upon a child around his first birthday, the latter following initiation. This procedure is followed to prevent the demon from eating the child. Roheim comments: "(T)his is a very clear instance showing how the mamu (demon) is derived from the parents, for actually the infant is in danger of being eaten by the parents, and this danger ceases when the child receives a name" (4:60).

Although the parents slay and devour the infant, they do not identify with this active role. They first seek by ritual to protect the child. They feel guilty about their act (husband performs ritual punishment, participants deny their cannibalistic partaking). In their dreams the act seems distasteful, and they are frightened. The demon is not themselves, but their mother. The equation is between the self as child-victim and the mother as aggressive devourer. "The child . . . represents its parents' parents . . . (T)his psychological reincarnation is proved by the fact that a child is named after its grandfather" (4:62).

We have, once again, the process of splitting internal experiences or intentions and dividing them among external imagos. The woman, in her experience of self as child, wishes to destroy and merge with the mother. The cultural image of the infant is that of a devouring, insatiable monster. These wishes are reversed, and in the transformation one's mother—the being from whom one wishes to wrest the cure for eternal discomfort—is experienced as malevolent. It is the "other" who wishes to steal from and destroy the self. This enhances the paranoid quality or structure the woman creates for herself. At the same time, the woman as mother is convinced that she is embattled and deprived. Overwhelmed by her hunger, she seeks to devour her own young, who have now become the merged symbol of both satiation and the threatening demon (i.e., one's own parents). These are, indeed, the essential characteristics of the other in the various permutations of the cultural drama. The other, be it parent or child, can somehow provide exquisite gratification. At the same time, it is dangerous; it is out to get the self and consume or smash it. The actor does not experience himself as greedy or cruel, but only self-protective and driven by fundamental need. The self is always the helpless victim, the one caught in the middle. The child-self fears the devouring parents. The mother-self feels the need for protection from its voracious infant. That these beliefs are based on the projection of inner desires seems inescapable.

We see repeated expression of the identification between self and the child imago in these cultural productions. We might keep this metaphor in mind while we contemplate the countless myths of this region which represent the child's murderous rage toward his parents. The mother and father are not perceived as people so much as "giants, cannibal ogres . . . demons. The males have huge testicles and penes; the females large breasts and large vaginas" (4:65). The self is always in the experiential position of being a child facing a world of huge adults. A typical myth of this genre is as follows:

A bankalanga lives with his wife, and with them lives a normal (*kunindjatu*) child whom they had stolen from its parents. They have a big hut with a partition in it. The male bankalanga sleeps on that partition (floor), but his wife and the child sleep on the ground below. Thus the bankalanga is hidden so that the child thinks that he is alone in the hut with his mother. She sends the child for rats, and when he comes back the bankalanga, who was always lying on the partition, stands up and she gives him the meat. One day the child says, "It is raining," It is not rain, but the urine of the bankalanga. The woman tells him to go to a big fire and get dry. But he can smell that it is urine. So he calls the bankalanga woman to go hunting with him. He hides in the bush, however, and sees the bankalanga man coming out of the hut and going back into it again. He sets fire to the hut and burns it up with the man bankalanga in it. The woman bankalanga finds her dead husband, puts his body in a wooden trough, and follows the boy's footsteps, weeping. The boy goes to the real people (*kunindjatu*). The real people kill and burn the female demon. The boy is then initiated and lives there always. (4:66)

The child in the story has been betrayed and misused. He has been separated from his "good" (natural) parents by theft. The bogus mother misuses his generosity and obedience. She literally takes the food out of his mouth, giving it to the monster-lover whom she has hidden from the boy. It is not simply an oedipal drama where the boy must destroy the father because he is blocking access to the desired female. Both parents are withholding and fraudulent. They do not live up to what parents should be. The boy has a right to be enraged. He has been denied his birthright. Hence, the slaying of the father becomes an act of vengeance and self-preservation. It is not the boy who is greedy for total gratification and monstrous in his intentions, but rather the parents. They have twice disrupted the boy's idyll, first in taking him from his "real" parents and again, when they reveal to him that he is not "alone in the hut with his mother." The symbol of the parental sin is intercourse. They gratify themselves and exclude the boy. The boy tries to deny this coitus but cannot; he cannot believe that urine is rain. The final equation between urine and semen is widely shared among the children of this culture.[12]

The boy in the myth is sent away to find a big fire; he is rejected. The final insult comes when he sees the man "coming out of the hut and going back into it again." The monster is violating the mother and must die. The mother herself has collaborated in the boy's betrayal and is also eradicated. This final act is dependent on the boy joining the society of men. Manhood is rebirth. It represents a repudiation of the first parents who have proved unworthy and dangerous. The fraternal function is to give the boy strength. The boy and his peers must confront the woman who was not a good enough mother: "The real people kill and burn the female demon" (4:66).

Initiation, the joining of the fraternity, thus lays out a strategy of existence, but one laden with ambivalence. The purpose of initiation is to bolster men, to shore them up against the threat posed by women. At the same time, it permits "children" to confront a world too large and dangerous for them. This can only be attempted through transformation. The male not only becomes a supermale with a phallic weapon, but also a hermaphrodite who has attained female powers. In this process the people of the tribe become bisexual wanderers. The wandering is a means of protecting the self from engulfment by the mother, but is also experienced as a deprivation. Men wander in the hopes of finding a nirvana. Repeatedly, however, the only end possible for the journey is death. The transformation itself, as with the Borroro, is felt to be a loss. It can only be seen as a loss or death of the self. The end of the journey, the failure of the quest, is inherent in its beginning.

The boys embark on their journey, and attempt to alter their beings, not only because of a longing for inner quietude, but also because of fear. They cannot accept the consequences of their own actions. Both the wandering and self-mutilation serve to increase the sense of deprivation and longing which triggered them. These results are then attributed to maternal malevolence.[13]

The purpose of the wandering is to end the wandering, to replace what has been lost. The symbolic replacement of the fraternity for the mother, tjuringa for penis, is never convincing. Women remain fearful objects because the men continue to wish for maternal union. The Borroro reunite with mother as they leave her by fitting themselves with the penis sheath (mother symbol). In Australia, the boy's foreskin is removed during the initiation ceremony. The symbols of the ritual indicate, *"that the foreskin is the child, which is put back into a mother symbol: at the same time that the child is separated from the mother, the foreskin is reintroduced into the mother"* (3:68). That is, the mother or mother surrogate swallows the foreskin as part of the ceremony.[14]

The ritual seems then to negate its own meaning. Initiation means to be reborn, to be freed from the mother. It is, at the same time, a total reuniting with the mother. The fantasized goal and the fantasized terror are one and the same; absorption, loss of boundedness, loss of self. The boys still seek that which they feel they have been deprived of: nurturant bliss without anxiety or longing. There is movement or symbolic transformation accompanying this circuitous venture. The boy's new self (penis) is not his real self, but an artificial one. After initiation, jeopardy of the symbolic penis, used to enter women, is not a danger to the "real" self.[15]

The boy, through initiation, is granted eternal immunity. The cost is that he cannot live as himself, and in fact exists in a living death. He must thenceforth act vicariously, through identification with the father; or as the agent of the father. Desire and consummation can no longer be felt as his own, but through identification with the father, who acts as the young man's surrogate.[16]

Father and son thus join together in a metaphoric project, the return to bliss, to narcissistic wholeness, in union with mother. The image which projects this wish is that of dual beings, locked in eternal copulation. Psychoanalytic doctrine holds these two beings to be father and mother, the image to be "the primal scene." Initiation makes the boy a participant in this scene, albeit his partaking is through the father.

In the final initiation ceremony, a chief carries two "tjuringas on his back, tied together with a hair string and decorated with birds' down . . . The double tjurunga is called Kwanjatara (two together) by the western Aranda."

The myth clearly makes one of these tjurungas male and the other female. We have said before that practically the only taboo is witnessing parental intercourse; we now add that the central mystery is *showing the parental intercourse.*

For one thing, we have the word *erkuindja*—stuck together. The word connects the ritual with the demon lore in which erkuindja means the copulating dogs in the air . . . They look like a pair of dogs copulating, joined together by the penis of the male inserted into the female's genitals. They are thus a married couple permanently copulating. When they bite, their victim is immediately *cut in two.* Lelil-tikutu (Pindupi) described how a hunter will often suddenly observe two dogs in the act of coitus. They are *titjiri punguta* (joined together). He thinks they are ordinary dogs and goes nearer to see them more clearly. Then he discovers that they are not dogs at all but two men. He must run at once; for the devils have a crooked stick charged with evil magic, and if they catch him he must die. The Pitjentara call them kunamurula (joined by the vagina); each of them is a man and a woman copulating but with their heads facing in opposite directions (i.e., like dogs).

The Matuntara data throw further light on the subject. According to them, the two dogs are joined in coitus and bite people into two parts. The male dog is called *mamara* (like the father) and the bitch *jakura* (like the mother). (4:81)

This is the primal scene transformed, a compromise. At one level of fantasy, the primal scene is a combat to death. The male must either spear and destroy the woman, or she will engulf and swallow him. The child is only an observer, cannot partake in the conquest or the feast. In the rearranged primal scene, there is no longer movement. Eternal coitus is eternal stalemate. All are incorporated and all are safe, the father and son merging with each other as they merge with the mother. The primal scene becomes polymorphous, perverse. Initiation is mutual bloodtaking, mutual fondling, a pile of male bodies.[17]

The triangle is completed. Mother, father, and son are welded together in hermaphroditic wholeness. The natural image which the Australians use to express this state is the Milky Way.

The Milky Way consists of two big *kuntanka* (tjurunga) standing crosswise. At Lingakura a boy of the ant totem was circumcised. When the women made the ceremonial dance for him, a demon woman came up and pulled his penis into her vagina, and there she held it fast with her labia. In this position, hanging on to each other, with the boy above, they ascended to the sky. The name of the Milky Way is therefore *ngatanuta*, i.e., stuck together (in coitus). There the two are stuck together in eternal intercourse. (3:65)

The little boy has been allowed to enter the scene because

he is no longer competing with the father, but has joined him, is acting for and with him. "What we now see is the transformation of the mother-child dual unity into a phallic dual unity—the heroes are Testicles and Semen or Father and Son, with the Son as the penis of the Father" (3:66).

On one level, each participant has partially fulfilled his aim. The mother has an unbreakable hold on husband and son, has indeed reincorporated her child into her womb, as she does in her cannibalistic devourings. Father and son have re-entered the mother, and need never leave. They are also now safe. The son can't be swallowed; he is now part of the powerful father. The father has also found immunity. He sends his penis-son into the arena as his agent.

Male-female hostility and parent-child antinomy have been mitigated. The actors have entered the imagos and become the monsters in the paranoid dream. In their unity, the participants have become the possessors of "evil magic"; they are the killers whose bite immediately cuts their victim in two. In the image of eternal coitus, each actor has survived through becoming the not-self, and through relinquishing movement. They are suspended in time.

The sense of absurdity of existence in culture is always two-edged. The self, in its constructions of reality and its attempts to act on the world, experiences its own absurdity. At the same time, the actor cannot but recognize the unreality of the collective myth. The primitive, through the undeniable quality of his own being, knows that he is not being "transformed" by his rites of passage. He knows this each night as he removes his plug on the way to the bush, or as he engages in intercourse with nothing but an erect penis. He is alienated from the reality he fosters.

The absurdity of one's own being and the absurdity of culture share a quality of desperation. Both the cultural and noncultural self are eternal wanderers, pursuing an unfulfillable quest. The essential, inescapable experience of the despairing self is recurrently found in the image of the abandoned or misused infant. In this metaphor, mother and father have everything, are everything, but will not share this bounty with the self. This metaphor, in its many variations, can only bespeak an abiding sense of being separated from fulfillment, from an inner sense of well being. In the metaphor of the infant, this nagging discomfort leads to desperation and rage. Nothing short of eating the mother alive or impaling her on a spear can relieve the internal torment.

One aspect of the absurdity of self is clearly portrayed by primitive peoples. Even devouring or impaling the mother— the outer limits of possible action—have no impact on the abiding sense of needful hunger. Such an act simply becomes one in a series of atrocities that change nothing. They are happenings in the context of endless wandering.

Another aspect of this bad faith is the abiding sense of innocence as moral justification, which the self seeks to maintain no matter how loathsome and greedy its actions. Theft is always experienced as retaking that which is rightfully yours, murder as just retribution or self-protection. Finally, the quandary of the cultural self is that it always experiences itself as being in the disadvantaged position. The self continually feels that the "other" (be it parent, spouse, or competitor) starts out in the power position and therefore feels free to utilize any means available to redress the balance.

The self, it would seem, can experience the absurdity of these feelings and beliefs, can fall out of the collective dream. The images of self as victim or baby can have an almost playful quality, wherein they are believed at one moment and discarded the next. Each actor retains the potential of seeing beyond his particular fictionalized account of himself in the world. This is the capacity to see one's own beliefs as absurd, the awakening perception of alienation. It is a sense of self outside of the absurd postulations. It is also true that the feelings of deprivation, fear, and incompleteness are deadly serious. They are linked with an abiding sense of inner pain which ebbs and wanes but does not disappear. This pain pushes the self to step out of the cultural dream.

In primitive culture the feelings of disquietude are crystallized into scenarios that are far less vague, fluid, and personal. The sense of being victim and underdog is manifest in the pervasive bifurcations we have seen in the myths and rituals. Men are at war with women; children are the natural enemies of adults; clan strives against clan. Each self of the duality is deprived in relation to the other. Men envy women's power to give birth and fear their mysteries. Women envy men for not having to bleed or be pregnant. Children covet the strength and size of adults, and feel excluded from their sexuality as the road of bliss. Adults portray infancy as nirvana, a state of nurturance where tension is unknown.

As we have seen, the absurdity of the caricatures that populate the cultural myth are clearly known to the players. The self that represents its total innocence of intent knows its own greed, its own callousness and occasional sadism. The ambivalence of these realizations riddle the cultures we are examining. The man, feeling menaced, becomes the menacing spear-thrower. This transformation is not simply a defensive reaction. It is also a portrayal of the experiential reality of his aggressive role and feelings in the sexual act. The "eyes turn away" maiden, embodiment of innocence, also plays out the classic role of seductress. She clearly knows that desire resides in her as well as in the male.

Culture, then, is seen as absurd by its participants because it cannot sustain its own mythic assertions. If the assertions themselves are absurd in their extremity, culture is also absurd in that each silly element is counterposed against its own negation. The scenario of culture is characterized by nonmovement. Each caricature is locked into a limbo of nonconquest. Each encounter between the devouring woman (snake) and excited male (spear-thrower) is a Mexican stand-off. Neither destroys, nor is destroyed, by the other.

The child may survive infancy but lives with a pervasive fear that he will be devoured. The mother may consume her child but is left with an internal emptiness called "meat hunger." Culture represents a war without resolution, fought by protagonists who are representations of one another and themselves.

It is in the context of this realization that the self yearns to step out of culture. If it is painful and frightening to be one's self, the price sometimes seems reasonable. In culture, in the imago of spear-thrower or "vagina dentata," the self often yearns for the simple relief of expressing the complexity of its own humanity. This expression may lead to disaster but is associated with a sense of aliveness and reality. Stepping out of culture is seen as waking up. Cultural existence is the experiental analog of eternal wandering in a dream.

Our original Borroro myth is no longer so puzzling. The boy is the cultural hero because of the mother rape, not despite it. The essential point is that he acts as himself, not as one who has undergone ritual death and is reincarnated as someone else's vassal. The father, like all men, identifies with the crime, which expresses shared longings. The son as the extension of the self acts out one's wish; as in the ritual, he represents one's penis. The mother is not outraged, but fulfilled. She has possessed her son and reintegrated him. She need not see her natural son die and repudiate her, as he does when initiated. She remains his magical object of fulfillment. Moreover, she is innocent of evil intent. She has been forced, is a victim rather than an evil devourer.

The saga of the myth expresses both the enactment of the forbidden and the imposition of controls. The punishment and wandering that follow the rape are a retreat, a defense against acting out the primordial wishes, against achieving the primordial image of bliss. In wandering, one moves away from that which he feels would make him complete only to seek that object in new forms. There is a patently self-delusive quality to this enterprise. There is no such object as is being sought, and there cannot be. Yet the self feels deprived and cheated because he cannot find the other who will end his longing. The wandering of the mythic hero is not only based on a lie (I have a giant penis, which is a weapon), it is also tantamount to living in a state of pain, of unfulfillment:

> (T)he myth describes a state of perpetual erection, a perpetual state of lust . . . here walking is genitalized, treated as if it were coitus. Malpunga is not the only great wanderer who is a phallic hero. Hermes, the god of roads, the protector of travellers and therefore the god of trade, the 'psychopompos,' the leader of souls into the Land of the Hereafter . . . the god of dreamland—Hermes is originally a phallic milestone. (3:11)

The walking of the wanderer is not an idyll but an endless trek leading nowhere. No act that the wanderer takes can lead to fulfillment, except the surrender to the snake which drags him "down into the earth." It is precisely this surrender which is ruled out by the terms of the myth. The hero's task is to fight his fate, to reject the one thing he finds alluring. The Milky Way is not a comforting or blissful image. It hangs suspended, revolving eternally in a dark void, seemingly without purpose. If the wandering is reunion with mother, it is in bondage rather than fulfillment.

> The dance of life, the whole story of our wanderings; in a labyrinth of error, the labyrinth of this world . . . (The wanderer flies) into the wilderness from the face of the dragon . . .
> The exodus is an initiation; the wandering is a rite of passage, from Troy to New Troy, from England to New England. From the mother to the mother; we are getting nowhere. And the wandering is all in the mother: the churinga which the initiate takes with him on the way, marked with the concentric maze pattern, symbolizes and magically achieves the unity of the infant with the mother. Thus 'they

always stay where they were born, so that the individual compelled by reality to eternal wanderings, in this his supernatural form has never left his mother.' (2:40–41)

The bondage is safety, but it is also—as the rituals have insisted time and again—death. Perhaps more precisely, it is a metaphoric refusal to experience one's life as having begun. The man in the cultural dream is in bondage, is waiting for time to begin. Until he is "free," nothing he can do counts; existence is unreal. These men, like Freud's patients, build and dictate their lives on recurrent ritual. This ritual itself is created from unreality; that is, it "really derived from dreams" (3:6). Not only does one enact what another might define as unreality, but he simultaneously recognizes it as such. Roheim reports that in one of his tribes, children often play a game called Altjira. In it the boy will designate a leaf as himself, another as his first wife, and so on. He then hits the leaves with a stick, rearranging them. The boy will interpret these shifting patterns of the leaves as a "future." The leaves falling together will be a fight or an alliance. When one blows away, it is a death or a separation. In this game the child evolves the fantasy of his own future (3:7). The daydream, the child's game, the fantasy—all are the script that men enact as their lives. They know this but nevertheless continue their enactments.

The rituals and myths we have been examining, the bad faith modality of culture, represent attempts to escape conflict over the self. They seem, however, to defeat their own purpose. Myth and ritual evolve into the metaphoric expression of eternal conflict. Built on the mundane, they are incredibly diverse and creative in blending both the negation and fulfillment of the wish. Culture, enacting this metaphor, becomes a suspension in time. The heroes of the myth prolong their pointless wandering; the only alternative envisioned is the seeking of death. Cultural actors stave off living as themselves in the hope of avoiding vulnerability. Yet they cannot avoid being partially alienated from their own enterprise.

Therein lies the second level of tension in the collective dream and the ritual. As modalities of experience, they negate that which the dreamers know to be true. Women must be raped but are really the seducers. Mothers wish to protect their infants, but eat them. Heroes want to survive, but blunder their way to doom. Action is always the negation of intent because, in the dream, the wanderer is never free to act as himself. Each man suffers from this unfreedom and the sham that he knows his bondage to be. His potential alienation, an assertion of liberation, is undercut by his fear of living as himself.

The dream, like the ritual, makes each actor the agent of someone else's will, some irresistible outside force. The struggle of existence is cast in the mode of resisting rather than being. Action is always against one's will, or as someone else. Intention is always disguised or distorted. The pattern established in the Borroro tale epitomizes much of the experience of self in culture, the experience of bad faith. Myth and ritual—the primary ingredients of culture—are enactments of the dream, are the concretization of fantasy. In the dream, one embarks on the journey of defending the self and ending the sense of deprivation. These goals are always unobtainable and are portrayed as mutually contradictory. The dream journey becomes a fight for survival. Survival demands theft and murder. The environment is filled with objects who possess that which the self craves, but who are reluctant to provide succor. These depriving others become monsters. Their intention is to empty the self, to enslave and destroy it. One is enmeshed in an exquisite dilemma. The self must approach the other to get what is necessary and desirable. In so doing, the self is put in danger of being seized and swallowed.

This dilemma, in defining the experience of being in the world, has several ramifications. It becomes unbearably perilous to act or live as one's self. Qualities, body parts, strength, and mysteries must be drawn from the world as armor and as weapons. One can never act freely. Compulsion, immediate threat, and the lust of others to control and possess the self are constant impingements. The self is left no choice but to flee and to fight, to be a soldier in his culture's "Army of Mars." The wandering of the dream of life is the only existence the dreamer knows. It is also experienced as unreal, as a preparation for living. The odyssey is an attempt to find some amulet or object that will both destroy the monsters and end one's sense of unfulfilled craving. Possessing this object is the precondition to becoming alive, to living freely as one's self. Alienation calls to the self to stop seeking this amulet and to simply attempt living without social protection.

The despair that culture represents is manifest. The cultural image of the liberating, perfect object also merges with the image of death. In the fantasy, that which the hero is running toward is also what he is running away from. The protagonist, the despairing self, does not know how to regard his own desires and his own fears. Bifurcating desire into longing and death, he is forever at war with himself. Projecting this cleavage onto the world, he is constantly striving against the weight of reality. Attempting to come to grips with the self through projection and metaphor, the actor always disbelieves his own creations. The sense of the absurd is the fragile barrier between self and fantasy, between self and culture.

Such is the quality of existence in culture, the same quality of existence that afflicts the rat man. It is this mode of being from which the patient, in decrying his madness, wishes to be free. The self in culture, like the patient, yearns to emerge from the dream yet fears this emergence. The experience of alienation is an irritant, a constant exhortation to resign from the collective, from Vonnegut's Army of Mars. At the same time it is an exhortation to recognize that, at precisely the moment of one's resignation, one will know oneself as the terrifying responsibility for being everything one is and can ever be or not be.

References

1. Bruno Bettelheim, *Symbolic Wounds*, New York, Collier Books (1952).
2. Brown, Norman O., *Love's Body*, New York, Random House (1966).
3. Roheim, Geza, *The Eternal Ones of the Dream,* New York, International Universities Press (1966).
4. Roheim, Geza, *Psychoanalysis and Anthropology*, New York, International Universities Press (1969).
5. Slater, Philip E., *The Glory of Hera*, Boston, Beacon Press (1968).

Epilogue: Alienation and the Myth of Culture

The symbolic productions of alienation—whether novel, myth, biography, song, or "symptom"—provide us with an image of reality, but they do not define human nature for us, nor do they prescribe a cure for the suffering of despair. The alienated experience negates the very possibility of such definitions and cures. This experience, as we have interpreted its manifold expressions, explores the modes of existence we have created for ourselves under the labels of "culture" and "society." Such modes of existence do not, the alienated tell us, represent the entire range of human possibility, but other possibilities can be known only by stepping outside the definitions of self provided by social reality. The alienated speak to us of the intolerable, self-negating aspects of existence in the matrix of social myth, but cannot tell us what we may become outside of this web.

Alienation represents an essentially negative language. It bespeaks the consequences of clinging to bad faith as one's essential mode of being in the world. The attempt to find safety in negating the self leads inevitably to the experience of pain and inner deadness. In becoming an object-self, part of an objective social history, the person can come to feel that he has lost control over his own being. These perceptions and feelings provoke despair. They do not necessarily lead the self to struggle against its bad faith nor to de-objectify itself. Bad faith, built on self-delusion, can feed on the very pain it generates. The escape from the feeling of deadness, the self strives to believe, is through culture. Culture will invest the self with new properties that will make it feel real and whole. In bad faith one works to insulate himself from the perception that this transformation is illusory. He continues existing in the expectation that his life will soon begin, will be the reward culture grants to him.

While struggling to retain an identity between one's possibilities and his cultural self, the person continues to glimpse the absurdity of his endeavor. These fleeting perceptions may be reacted to in a variety of ways. For the "middle Americans" and the Chaga, they remain no more than momentary diversions. The sense of absurdity does not require one to give up belief in culture, it merely challenges that belief. For others, the sense of absurdity and pain associated with bad faith seems to puncture their immediate reality. They take it as a signal that they must seek some sense of self which lies outside of what culture invites them to be.

It is this quest to experience the self as something other than an imago that we have characterized as the journey into silence. Silence represents an attempt to remove the self from the ongoing cycle of enacting depersonalized roles for the other while they reciprocate in kind. To use Sartre's example, it is a refusal to do the dance of the waiter and to exist as a waiter-thing.

This journey requires one to separate, at least temporarily, from the ground of culture. The self, even in profound alienation, remains conflictually drawn back to the collective as a source of strength. Herzog hides in Ludeyville and Invisible Man in his basement as they seek to cure themselves of the affliction of bad faith. Their quest dissolves their historical identity. It removes them from the ongoing drama that culture enacts. Since only object-selves are recognized by culture, such withdrawal requires the self to become invisible. This quest for invisibility is the ultimate negation of culture.

We should emphasize that negating culture is not identical to negating human contact. As Cleaver emphasizes, men in culture can live out much of their lives without ever seeing or touching each other. They deal only with the imagos or object-selves in which men try to lose themselves. For some, it is the desperately felt need to be seen as themselves and to see others in their humanity which impels their negation of culture.

Let us attempt to characterize the central themes and perceptions of the alienated experience.

Alienation as Dreaming

There are many commonalities in the alienated perception of the plight of self in culture. First, existence in culture seems to demand that the self adopt a mythic modality; that one assume a stance of bad faith. This involves, both for each self and for the collective, generating a fantasy structure that categorizes all experience. Within this structure, one's own being in the world and one's conception of the other become objectified and delimited. Persons become objects whose fate it is to enact their part in the collective drama. This leaves the self with a legacy of discontent. One continues to vacillate between belief in the fantasy structure as the only possible reality and a rejection of culture as both unreal and intolerable. Culture is not only an attempt to define reality in a particular way, but also an attempt to deal with the tension and anguish that goes along with the maintenance of these definitions.

We have tried to explore these themes in our excursions into psychiatry and anthropology. In looking at structures different from our own, we can more easily appreciate the ways in which men construct their images of the world. Far from being "given" by the nature of reality, the particular metaphors that organize diverse cultures seem to be imposed on the world with an apparent disregard for data. They are also clung to with a tenacity that makes them almost unshakable. Those we call madmen seem to illustrate the same process.

179

Their interpretations of reality appear to be largely fixed: the world does no more than provide raw material which can be molded or distorted or coerced into justifying a preexisting mental structure.

In these mythic structures—whether individual or collective—each actor assumes that it is his fate to be "fulfilled." We have seen multiple images of what this fulfillment would entail. It is commonly a picture of perfect bliss: the fantasied position of the infant merged with a perfect, all-giving mother. This ideal "other" would respond immediately to all needs, would banish any possible discomfort before it could even be felt—in brief, would make the experience of the self perfect. Since no infant has ever known this experience, the yearning for it can hardly be called a regression. It would seem to be, instead, a projection or fantasy of what the self feels it deserves. The self demands that it experience all it seems to lack in its current existence. It demands to feel whole, to feel alive, to feel secure and protected, to feel courageous and capable, to experience a sense of inner strength which will permit it to subdue the world. If one cannot achieve infantile bliss, one seeks to become an all-conquering person, the child of God, and to be given wealth and beautiful things. The experience of being a perfect self is pursued with moral outrage. Each protagonist sees a perfect self as his birthright, as something stolen from him by the world. Regardless of what the self achieves or acquires, it is left with a feeling of having been short-changed. An inner craving persists, a feeling that the self has something more coming to it.

Even while feeling that culture, "the world," is partially "to blame"—that it is conspiring against the self or failing to appreciate one's legitimate demands—each person expresses the belief that he can be fulfilled only through culture. Yearning to be strong and brave, the self feels puny and cowardly in the face of an oppressive reality. It seeks to draw strength from others. Only by joining the "community," the storehouse of valuables by which the self can be transformed, can the self hope to realize its "fate" of reaching nirvana.

Freud's patients demonstrate, in idiosyncratic terms, the same belief. Other men hold the key to one's well being. If the self is to have that which it deserves, it must wrest that amulet from the other. The rat man experiences his life as misery because of his dead father, because of his fiancée, because of "the captain" or because of the chance remarks of the railroad porter. Patients in turn seek to end their sense of oppression through enlisting the aid of others: the rat man throws himself on Freud and demands that the therapist give him all he needs.

Madmen demand salvation from others in ways that are deemed by society as unacceptable, which is the reason society calls them madmen. To be sane, as defined by the culture, is to make such demands but according to the rules of the collective game. Within the culture one pays the price for his transformation by making himself obedient to cultural dicta. One turns himself into a part of something that is larger than, and outside of, himself: one seeks to become part of history. This is Invisible Man's quest. By becoming part of history he hopes to transcend the condition of his slavery, of his being a nigger. He begins his quest feeling unworthy, confused, and unborn. He assumes that he will begin to feel whole, certain, and valuable once he has found his appropriate place in history. The middle Americans feel unfulfilled because history will not recognize them; "they don't listen to us" is their lament. Seeing history as the only path to the realization of its fate, the self attempts to shape its very being to the demands of history. The self seeks to become the object described in the scenario of culture. Invisible Man wishes fervently to become a leader of his race, to become another Bledsoe. Herzog seeks a place in history through the creation of new dogma which can order men's lives. Rumfoord would become a God, would tamper with history in an attempt to dispel his own ennui. Cleaver and Hoffman find history the obstacle to liberty and must battle against it in order to feel virtuous and free.

Invisible Man's dream bespeaks the ambivalence of pursuing a place in history. The attempt to transform one's self into an imago or an object in the historical drama is no more than an endless pursuit of a phantom; it is being a "nigger boy" who is always kept running. Goffman's observations seem to tell us that this view of social reality is not mere hyperbole. Many people experience their relationship to their own behavior in precisely these terms. They feel like imposters who can never become what they pretend to be, yet they keep running and running for the chance to occupy new and better personas in which they feel equally awkward and discontented.

This modality of existence, this conflicted yearning for a place in history, is carried on though a continual discourse. The self keeps seeking contact with others that it might hear their demands and present a persona to them for their approval. Invisible Man's yearning to give his graduation speech to those who might judge him is a representation of this kind of talk. He yearns to hear their reaction to him so that he will know what to become, and how he should feel about himself. He yearns to absorb all the images others have of him, all their ideas of what he should become, and to make his life the enactment of those visions. He acts as if he must be told what he must do to have his wishes granted.

Herzog forthrightly tells us that his self had become "a collective project." More specifically he, like Invisible Man, had delivered himself over to others that he might be cured. It is not simply that he feels helpless in the face of the collective. Herzog's acquiescence, like Invisible Man's, is also an implicit demand. Each man feels certain that, if he will only shape himself into the kind of object which others value, he will clearly be rewarded for his obedience. This reward represents, in their fantasies, the achievement of that perfect self each man feels to be his birthright and his fate. Herzog will become the hero who conquers and possesses the beautiful Madeline, the genius who provides the answers to ameliorate the misery of modern man. Invisible Man will have "not one, but two Cadillacs, a good salary and a soft, good looking and creamy complexioned wife." They keep sacrificing more and more in the way of obedience to others in order to achieve these rewards. Their commitment to achieving these goals, to becoming the heroic imago which history can revere, becomes the very center of their being in the world. At the height of their frenzy to join history, they can sense nothing else: they will either win their perfection in the collective or be nothing. Doubts about the reality of this project and revulsion at the price it exacts are pushed aside. It becomes almost unthinkable that one's sacrifices may have been in vain. Feeling debased by their obeisance to the collective and waiting expectantly for their just deserts, our protagonists cling desperately to their belief in culture.

The maintenance of this belief is compounded of hope and fear. The self discovers, with great frequency, that history provides no more than brass tokens and pain. Even knowing this, one can apparently still find the prospect of straying from culture's path quite unimaginable. The self clings to the hope that the next battle will be the final test, the last humiliation. The self will have finally demonstrated its worth. History will begin providing all those things one has earned, the "fate" that one has always deserved. Somewhere, the self works to believe, culture really has a storehouse of gold coins that can make one truly rich. These hopes—no matter how naive— begin to appear and receive bolstering from one's terror over considering the alternatives. If the self loses faith in culture's rewards, it faces the prospect of falling out of history.

Our protagonists express the fear that leaving history is tantamount to being obliterated. Having tried to become alive through finding a place in history, they fear that giving up the project of finding recognition will mean that they can no longer be human. They can envision nothing except terror and loneliness should they reject the collective endeavor. The misery of endless drudgery and repeated disappointment may seem preferable to facing the unknown. The unknown becomes—in their imagining of it—filled with vague and terrifying contents. Giving up belief in history is seen as the door into madness, an excursion into a wilderness where the self will be lost and unprotected, a reversion to being no more than a beast. The self fears that it can only remain visible, can only become human, by following the script that culture provides. Counterposed to these fears is both a self loathing and a sense of absurdity which helps one to "see" what he is doing to himself.

Alienation as Seeing

Open to the experience of alienation, one senses the futility of his eternal struggle and the madness of the beliefs that support it. These beliefs are seen as leading the self into the enactment of futile scripts. These circular, never-ending scenarios exist, as we have seen, not only on the personal level of that which a self enacts, but also as the collective definitions men give to reality. Such metaphors are the cultures that men build in the name of adapting to the world. The enactments of these definitions, the alienated declare, are the rituals of social interaction, the basis of what men in culture regard as sanity.

From Vonnegut through Hoffman and Cleaver, to the middle Americans, to Herzog and Invisible Man, to the participants in what we call primitive cultures, this is the initial, focal perception which leads to a new appreciation of reality: men act collectively to construct their lives on ridiculous, mad, absurd foundations. They define reality in whatever way deemed necessary to justify their acts, and "disallow" divergent definitions by relegating them to such categories as madness. This awakening perception of alienation comes with a recognition of collective beliefs as pseudo-reality, which, in Vonnegut's imagery is a recognition that society can be experienced as an Army of Mars. Each man can only pretend—to himself and others—that he comprehends a meaning and a purpose behind what he is doing. The Army of Mars acts, in the name of righteousness, to turn each man into a robot, a victim of unseen forces, and a murderer. Each soldier inflicts pain upon the others and controls them, even as he suffers pain and feels himself to be controlled. Each is simultaneously an agent and a victim of suffering. In Hoffman's imagery, Eichmann is the perfect representation of this mode of existence.

Unk, Boaz, and Stony represent another part of each automaton—that element of his being which Invisible Man calls the "grandfather part" of himself. This component of the self is the will to resist, the unending potential to see the fraudulent quality of collective acts. Only by seeing in this particular alienated way do our protagonists find a premise that permits them to be other than robots. This premise, an appreciation of one's humanity outside of the demands of the collective myth, underlies the refusal of Unk, Boaz, and Stony to be controlled, and their refusal to act destructively to others. Cleaver "sees" the mad mythology of racism, and his own place in it, and can then renounce his own behavior as a rapist. His humanity depends, he comes to realize, on the refusal to rape as much as it demands his refusal to shuffle. Herzog can only begin to awaken from the dream when he gives up the project of vengeance against Gersbach and Madeleine. Invisible Man withdraws from the dreams of others only after confronting Ras as "the destroyer," now bent on waging a war on all whites. Invisible Man rejects this project, seeking his humanity in something other than the holy crusade Ras represents; a crusade grounded in "hatred and a confusion over the nature of reality."

This act of seeing, of knowing the absurdity of what men

collectively regard as inevitable, may be irreversible. Our protagonists seem to illustrate that, once having experienced culture from the alienated perspective, one can never again become totally committed to the collective. One might, like Invisible Man, wish mightily to re-enter the dream. Yet he finds within himself a continual vulnerability, a potential to phase out of the dream. Invisible Man describes his initial awakening as "a remote explosion . . . it had caused the ice cap to shift the slightest bit. But that bit, that fraction, was irrevocable" (1:226).

To move into the alienated position would thus seem to be an act that changes the very quality of one's being. It does not, however, determine what paths the self will subsequently pursue. The movement into alienation may give one a sense of clarification, but it provides no answers. Indeed, the alienated protagonist discovers new levels of anguish as the collective world becomes less substantial for him. He discovers, like Malachai Constant, or Cleaver or Herzog, that he has helped to create the nightmare that he finds so loathsome. Moreover, this predilection for creating a dream existence does not simply disappear in the act of becoming alienated. Our protagonists show a potential for creating a new type of drama in which they are good, innocent, and noble. They feel compelled to do battle with culture as their minotaur, and to awaken those slumberers still enmeshed in the dream. Some, like Hoffman and Cleaver, seem to find it difficult to move beyond this position. Others, like Herzog and Invisible Man, seek to exorcise this more personal bad faith. They attempt to live without either the myth of culture or a personal, self-justifying myth in which they stand in opposition to culture. This attempt to give up the crusade of reform, of social change, is the more agonizing struggle which the alienated vision may eventually precipitate.

At the least, a common vision emerges in all the representations of alienation. In all its manifestations, alienation bespeaks a fundamental antinomy between the self and culture.

In creating social definitions of reality, in prescribing ritual, in establishing institutional forms that differentiate men hierarchically and regulate their relations to one another, men create the basis of their own feelings and non-humanness. To give one's self over to culture, the alienated declare, requires distorting the experience of being and negating the foundations of the self.

This antinomy is portrayed as fundamental. It is not particular cultures or institutions which are experienced as absurd, but the very forms themselves. To the degree that one stands within a culture and defines himself through a culture's categories, he exists as an imago. Nevertheless, the self, our anti-heroes tell us, clings desperately to its imago existence, to its own self-negation. There is, at least in the first instance, relief to be found in the possibility of living as a stereotype. Culture can be used to ameliorate the ambiguity of having to know the self, of facing the world, and choosing one's own path. Culture advertises itself as embodying wisdom. To follow its dictates is to be directed toward fulfillment. Men yearn to believe that this is true; to believe the answers have been compiled and that they need only absorb them to find some sort of salvation. The alienated also cannot help experiencing that their salvation is never forthcoming, that the answers found in culture are macabre jokes. This can be not only an enraging but also a very frightening perception. If one falls out of his belief in collective wisdom, he can feel betrayed, misused, and without direction. The self can, in these moments, experience extreme terror. Culture, to which the self has clung to ensure its preservation, seems to evaporate like a chimera. Perhaps equally terrifying is that this "awakening" demonstrates to the alienated that they heretofore have deluded themselves into believing a mad fiction. How can they regain a belief in their own perceptions having once experienced the possibility of their own bad faith? The criteria for viewing reality seem to become, for the alienated, both more experimental and less fixed. That is, the alienated are left with a continued sense of suspicion that they may be deluding themselves, that any perception of the self or other must be open for reassessment. This puts a great burden on the self. It dissolves the possibility of moral certainty. One can only, like Herzog and Invisible Man, seek to monitor his "stomach," seek to come into contact with those inner signals which tell the self when it is moving into or out of the dream. One can, it seems, become aware of those modalities in which he feels more or less alive, more or less like himself rather than a manifestation of some collective fantasy.

This possibility seems to underlie the positive hope which surfaces along with the disillusionment of alienation. If culture is no more than a myth, one can be free of it; the self can stand on its own. If one can experience his own bad faith and his predilection to collude with others, this can represent the first step in a disengagement from myth. In those moments of awakening from the dream, our protagonists speak to us of experiencing elation. They glimpse the possibility of freedom, of becoming something for which no model yet exists.

Those experiences which signal one's alienation, despair and a sense of the absurdity of existence in culture, seem to recur in many times and many places. The self may first locate its despair in the particular circumstances of its existence. As one moves through different roles and different segments of the culture, he may come to appreciate alienation itself as the essential quality of his relation to the collectivity. This is the common journey that recurs in all of our statements of alienation. It is the outcome of Malachai Constant's travels through time and space, the Band's drive for success, Cleaver's quest for vengeance and supremacy, Hoffman's revolutionary enterprise, Herzog's attempts to reorder his life, the middle American's efforts to get ahead, and Invisible Man's search for a place in history. Each alienated self finds that the fight to end his despair has been misdirected. Each begins his combat with a particular segment of the world, a particular aspect of the collective fantasy that he finds unbearable. As their initial battle proves fruitless, the alienated move toward an understanding that it is the dream *quality* of his existence which generates his despair, rather than the content of the dream in which he is immersed. Alienation penetrates and subverts the fantasies and visions which the self constructs in its efforts to define the world. Alienation continually informs the self of the unreality of these myths and dreams.

Alienation as Awakening

Alienation is the experience of striving to negate the fears and hopes that keep the self enmeshed in culture. Culture, as a myth, creates a vision of the world. Alienation turns this world upside down and dissolves it. This is the theme of alienation we have referred to as awakening. To awaken is to sense the absurdity of the myth one is enacting, to know it as a fabrication. The dream of finding life, integrity, and pleasure through culture is recognized as a nightmare. Culture, rather than protecting the self from the diffuse terror of nonbeing, is in fact that modality which produces the dreaded condition. The self, in its wish to guarantee its invincibility, attempts to enact a persona that will provide protection. To be alienated is to sense that one inevitably experiences inner death in trying to shape his self into such an object. If one wishes to feel alive, he would have to venture to live as himself.

This perception is not confined to the most radical moments of disengagement from the collective. As we have seen, the suspicion that culture is a fraud, that life is a carnival, pervades the existence of many. We struggle with this suspicion constantly but cannot bring ourselves to the point of acting on it. Just as the primitives laugh at their most sacred myths and debunk their communal preoccupations, so do we often know our belief in culture to be unfounded. This is part of the tension of living in bad faith and in collusion. We are fearful of taking our misgivings too seriously, of sharing them too vocally, lest the whole fabric of culture dissolve. Men in culture tiptoe around their unbelief as if their existence were dependent on maintaining a house of cards. At the same time, men in history seem haunted and fascinated by the possibility of negating the myth of culture. Both directly and indirectly, they speculate about discovering the possibilities that lie outside of the collective.

Carlos Castaneda's books, describing his experiences as an apprentice to a Yaqui "sorcerer," have become bestsellers. At the center of the old man's teachings lies the image we have encountered so often. It is the image of seeking to remove one's self from the communal discourse in order to feel in touch with the world; the image of being able to live one's own existence rather than enacting the dreams of others. It is the image of moving into that silence in which one stops asking culture for definitions of what he wants to be. For the Indian, this movement out of the collective image of the world requires one to become a "warrior." He advises Castaneda, who avowedly wishes to "see" the world:

> You talk to yourself too much . . . Everyone of us does that . . . we talk about our world. In fact we maintain our world with our internal talk . . . We renew it, we kindle it with life, we uphold it with our internal talk. Not only that, but we also choose our paths as we talk to ourselves.
> Thus we repeat the same choices over and over until the day we die, because we keep on repeating the same internal talk over and over until the day we die.
> "A warrior is aware of this and strives to stop his talking." (3:263)

This is a precaution about the hardships of becoming a warrior, of seeking to become one's self. Having lived in bad faith, the self has become addicted to the cultural image of reality. Answers found in the communal dialogue can seem to be the only possible answers. There is a sense of safety in listening to the collective voice. That voice provides the images that foreclose reality. It works to block out all other possibilities and make it possible for one never to have to regard himself, to be eternally oblivious to the signals of his own stomach. In the awakening of alienation, one wishes to finally silence that voice, to shut out the communal discourse. The alienated self seeks to experience its existence and to see the world as it might appear to him through other glasses. To be alienated is to rid one's self—at least partially—of the vision that existence outside of history is death. Alienation is an acceptance of the knowledge that it is life in history which shapes experience into a terrifying deadness.

Silence, that movement out of the discourse which joins one to history, is the opening up of new possibilities. This movement does not guarantee an end to one's suffering, nor even an end to one's bad faith, but it does move the self to a struggle which it can experience as more real. This new struggle is the attempt to know (as Invisible Man puts it) that part of one's sickness which he carries inside of him, that internal disquietude which the self seeks to place in the outer world. In silence the despairer can at least become aware of his own bad faith. He can recognize the ways in which he has seduced himself and other men into his fantasies while being seduced into theirs. Silence is a turning away from this mutual destructiveness. Stepping outside of history does not magically ensure one's "fate." It does bespeak the knowledge that culture cannot provide that certain cure.

The self, outside of history, may continue to generate fantasies about its fulfillment. These fantasies can, however, be recognized as such. They can be lived with, experimentally, as part of the pursuit of becoming one's self. In this pursuit, the alienated tell us, one feels uncertain, lonely, and somewhat afraid. Yet one also feels a sense of being alive that he has never known in pursuing the myths of culture. In silence there is no voice which claims one's attention and obedience with the promise of turning the self into something more than it has ever been. Alienation, Invisible Man declares, is the realization that one is nobody but himself. Moreover, that self is something which one possesses for himself. The other cannot dictate the experience of being in the world any more than he can make that experience nirvana. If the self would resist the modality of bad faith, it would have to accept an existence of uncertainty. The pursuit of certainty—be it through history or through a more personal bad faith—can only plunge the self back into another nightmare. This is the principle which the rat man so clearly exemplifies. He attempts to construct a reality that locates his suffering in a specific feature of the outer world, and attempts to create a ritual that will surely end his pain.

Freud's patients express the desire to change; they feel trapped by their internal talk. They continually castigate themselves and renounce the unrealities they create. These despairers remain, however, too conflicted and fearful ever to give up their dream existences. They move, instead, from symptom to symptom, each being an enactment of the same basic fantasies. Their internal talk, their recitations to their analyst, represent the fused product of both the suffering with this unreality and the unwillingness to relinquish it. In their internal talk they declare their own bad faith and bemoan the suffering associated with it. At the same time, they tell themselves that they are helpless to do anything but exist in their own nightmare. They express the feeling that they have not created the nightmare that plagues them, but are in fact its victim. They use talk to separate themselves from their own creations, from the choices they have made and the feelings they have experienced. Freud becomes magical for them, becomes "the healer." He is the one who holds the key to what can release them from their suffering. Freud used the understated label of "transference neurosis" in describing the particular unreality in which his patients attempted to envelop him. This so-called "transference neurosis" contains many of the elements that have become familiar to us. The patient feels himself to be confronting an imposing reality (the therapist as father, the therapist as omniscient). He or she is David face to face with Goliath. This other possesses everything that the self needs to feel fulfilled. They become desperate for Freud to give them these supplies. They feel that they can no longer tolerate their suffering and eternal longing. The patient becomes enraged because the therapist has failed him. The therapist must be either a monster or an imposter. If he has anything to give, why is he withholding it? If he has nothing to offer, why has he acted to generate expectations?

As they try to conceptualize their plight, ostensibly to become more aware of themselves, these patients recapitulate their bad faith. Therapy becomes another situation for them to bemoan. They are suspended in their misery but the fault, they feel, is not their own. Should they move toward "improvement," they would feel such change to be the gift of the therapist. Better or worse, they still experience themselves as the victims of the reality that surrounds them. Their well being is dependent on the other, and the other can never be sufficiently giving. The patient, Freud indicates in "Analysis Terminal and Interminable," leaves therapy much as he enters: longing for something from outside himself that will transform him (2:350–57).

Yet the goal of psychoanalysis was, as Freud conceived it, to move the patient beyond this point. In sitting behind the prone patient, being invisible and often silent, the analyst dramatizes for him another possibility. The patient is given the chance to experience the terms by which he—rather than others—constitutes his own reality. The therapist, in this sense, is neither withholding nor generous. He is no more than a screen on which the patient projects his own image of the world. At moments in the analysis almost all patients sense this essential fact of their situation. They learn, at least ideally, that the therapist is not the source of their fear and pain, and likewise is not the force that will cure them. Madmen can be maddeningly sane in this regard: they can and do come out of their delusions. Analysis often can be the setting for such moments of clarity, but of course the awakenings are not dependent on the ritualized situation. Time and again the patient, or any human being, senses the possibility of shedding his delusions. This sort of realization forms the essence of Vonnegut's world view, of Invisible Man's and Herzog's excursions, and of Hoffman's and Cleaver's exhortations. It is that sense of the absurd which can act as a wedge between the self and the myths that would enshroud it.

Silence and the Struggle to Find New Paths

We have heard a number of exhortations and claims that the appreciation of the absurd can form the basis of other modes of being. Even appreciating the dream quality of life in culture, the self does not move readily toward exploring these new modes. It is not, apparently, one's sense of the madness of collective structures which leads him heroically to renounce history. Rather, it is the despair, the pain, the sense of not being alive in culture which propels the self toward the alienated position. Malachai Constant, Cleaver, Herzog, Invisible Man, and our middle Americans all seem to undergo continual batterings in their imago existence. These beatings create in them a sense of desperation. Stepping outside of history becomes a less fearful prospect as the self gains more profound appreciation of the pain of being in history.

This pain is experienced, moreover, as unnecessary. The self gains an appreciation that culture provides only greater or lesser humiliation—pain or an absence of pain, but never those feelings of freedom, vitality, and joy that one is seeking. Alienation is a recognition that the self can never win freedom by enslaving itself to history. The self, as it is experienced in alienation, is free. One can either choose to act on that freedom and thus realize it or choose to act as if the freedom must come from somewhere else: from one's therapists, from the recognition of culture, or by some heroic conquest of monstrous forces.

The self can seek to experience this freedom by exploring the possibilities of silence. One cannot know the results of this exploration before it is begun. Those who have talked about alienation as fundamental to human existence provide many speculations about what lies on the other side of silence. Norman O. Brown declares that if we would only step outside of history, we would know eternal joy in the delights of the body re-experienced in all its vividness. Sartre invokes the belief that man can create his own existence in whatever terms he chooses, limited only by the situation of existence itself. Freud's vision is more somber: man will remain forever plagued by his internal conflicts and by his craving for options and objects that cannot be his. Freud believes that one must learn to live with his own disquietude, with a certain stoic grace. Kierkegaard, on the other hand, would have us believe that movement out of myth—collective and individual —will let us know God.

These speculations are themselves mythic. We do not and can not know what silence, what the end of history, will do for each man. The decision to move away from culture must be intensely personal. The self can hope that certain feelings and experiences will emerge from his encounters with himself; it cannot enter silence with the certainty of achieving these experiences. The belief in such certainties would make silence no more than another dream, and one that can never fulfill its promise. The movement into silence is visible only as an alternative. It may represent the only option the self can envision if it would resist joining an eternal struggle that absorbs all possibility and leaves one in an agony of emptiness that welcomes death itself. Perhaps silence will leave the self with an equal dose of pain, even a more personal dose, which cannot be blamed on the world. Perhaps it will provide the self with a willingness—or even an eagerness—to begin living as itself. Many voices in our culture are saying that this gamble seems worth while.

Whether disengagement from history is preferable to bad faith is thus a moot point. Alienation is not a new religion exhorting us to a promised land. It is a way of looking at our experiences in culture, and it may be clarifying. We are used to assuming that all positive experience and all that we value as human—imagination, the relation of man to man, art, music—are the gifts of culture. We tend to fear that, outside of the historical modality that judges each man and assigns him a place, all that we value will dissolve. Alienation dwells upon those moments of silence each man knows in his own life, and tells us that such moments are rife with possibility. To step into silence does not require one to stop thinking, to give up language, or to stop trying to build human relationships. Silence is a shutting off of the dialogue by which the self defines itself through culture's edicts and culture's response to him. Each man has experienced moments in which social definitions mean nothing to him, where the act is something he chooses without any expectation that it will evoke a response. These acts can contribute nothing to one's persona, to one's place in history, but they may have a very intense meaning to the self. Some may find these moments either irrelevant or fearful. Others may find in them an appreciation of a self which is not an imago and find in them possibilities that lie outside of history.

References

1. Ralph Ellison, *Invisible Man*, New York, Signet Books (1947).

2. Sigmund Freud, "Analysis Terminable and Interminable," *Collected Papers*, 5, New York, Basic Books (1959).
3. Carlos Castaneda, *A Separate Reality: Further Conversations with Don Juan*, New York, Simon and Schuster (1971).

Notes

Introduction

1. This general usage is most clearly paralleled in the existential-phenomenological tradition. It is expounded by such writers as Heidegger, Tillich, Sartre, and Laing. We will not attempt any detailed examination of the many differences between them.

2. For a fuller description of these varieties of despair, see Kierkegaard, *The Sickness unto Death* (6).

3. The films of Fellini, Bergman, and Cassavetes surely centered on these themes, as did much of the "living theater," the lyrics of Bob Dylan and the Band, and the novels of Joseph Heller, Kurt Vonnegut, Bruce Jay Friedman, and Harry Crewes.

4. See, for example, K. Kenniston, *The Uncommitted* (5) or J. Israel, *Alienation: From Marx to Modern Sociology* (4) for representative statements of how alienation has been viewed in psychology and sociology. See also R. Schacht, *Alienation* (8), for a general review of the usage of the term.

1. A Culture of Discontent

1. Vonnegut continues to underscore the absurdity of social hierarchies by having his army peopled by generals who are

front men. Secret commanders retain their anonymity by re-
maining enlisted men with hidden electronic devices to activate the officers' antennae.

4. Madness and Despair

1. It is not our intention, in this chapter, to contend with
or add to the various interpretations and revisions of Freud's
work. Whatever else his work may mean in some larger sense,
his case studies clearly provide a way of inquiring into the
human struggle over despair. It is solely in the spirit of that
inquiry that we approach one of his cases.

2. It is true that the father advised the patient to "stay
away" from the woman on the basis that he "would only
make a fool of himself" (3:59). However, this can most
easily be heard as friendly advice rather than patriarchal injunction. Most anyone but the patient himself could see that
the woman was not likely to return his ardor. The rat man's
slavish dedication would, indeed, turn him into a laughing
stock or an object of pity.

6. Culture as Absurdity

1. Paradoxically, Roheim points out, the subincision ceremony makes men more vulnerable to the problem of penis
captivus. It has the effect of making the erect penis broader
than it would otherwise be. "Possibly," Roheim concludes, the
often expressed fear of having the penis swallowed up in
coitus represents "a disguised wish for eternal pleasure" (4:
116).

2. This fear of a woman taking the penis has even earlier
roots (preceding initiation). Myth holds that a dreamer, if
he sees a phallic woman ("alknarintja") coming toward him,
must immediately awaken. This female monster will osten-

sibly force "a man to lie on his back and she will then sit on his penis" (4:68). The alknarintja will force the man to engage in coitus; she will play the male role in the superior position while he must "play the part of the female" (3:68). It is interesting to note that the feared phallic woman of the dream will come in the guise of a taboo woman. The ensuing intercourse is thus incestuous as well as "unnatural" (sex roles reversed). These fearful dreams apparently spill over into behavior and say something about women's intentions. One woman of this tribe reports to a field worker that "in her dream she had been chased by her brother. When she woke up from the incest dream she found that she was lying on top of her son nyiki. After this I began to make further inquiries and I soon found that this was regarded as the typical way for a mother to lie on her child. They even added, to make things clearer, that she lies on the child like the male on the female in cohabitation. . . . As a matter of fact, coitus in the inverted position is sometimes practiced, but the men say they are afraid to do it because their penis might break off" (4:68).

3. Slater has demonstrated the frequent slippage between one "threat" and the other, and the recurrence of the images of the enveloping female or vagina dentata. The specific form of this image of female greed and malevolence is often the serpent. "The snake appears far more often in mythology as a devouring than as a penetrating being, and when dragons appear in pairs, the female is almost always the more formidable of the two . . . Since the snake lives by devouring small beings, traditionally interpreted as symbolic either of phalli or children or both (Freud, 1900, pp. 357–358), it does indeed symbolize a 'dangerous vagina' as Roheim suggests. The 'danger' arises, however, because the serpent, whether viewed as a genital or not, is orally defined, and the fear which it evokes is of being absorbed by the mother, of being poisoned, or enveloped, or strangled—all common schizophrenic fantasies . . ." (5:87)

Innumerable myths echo this schizophrenic conception. The female monster or snake is the symbol of "the entangling, smothering, devouring mother who destroys the boundary between the child and the external world and returns him to a quiescent state of nonbeing" (5:88).

4. Roheim notes: "The pubic tassel is worn to hide the hole, not the penis. It is especially considered a great shame for the women to see the wound. The one thing that women are not allowed to do is to catch hold of the glans penis. If an uninitiated man cursed an initiated one with reference to the subincision wound ('Your subincision wound is big'), he was punished by death" (4:119).

The tjuringa is the major prop of the male rites in Australia. It is an artificial phallus bestowed upon the initiate by the group. It is said to represent the penis of a mythical warrior, the inventor of love magic. "The penis of this hero was in perpetual erection and his own penis was his tjuringa" (3:85). To own the tjuringa is to own a perpetual erection. A common feature of numerous initiation rites is the male dance carried out in a context of fearfulness in the face of women. Women have become, in their fiction, terrible monsters.

5. The women of this tribe are observed to "frequently act as the seducer, instead of the one who submits passively to violence. Like her sisters in other lands she can be a coquette and she knows very well how to use her eyes . . . Turning her head this way and that way, winking from the corner of her eye, she shows that she is willing. When the man comes nearer and talks to her she shakes her hips to excite him. She may open and close her legs (*mampatintum, Luritja*), imitating coitus movements. Some women like to tease men; they lie on their backs, show the vagina, and when the men get excited they refuse to grant their desires" (4:117).

6. The behavior which follows the transfer of the child is described in this manner. The husband-to-be behaves like an affectionate father, fondling the little girl, feeding her tidbits and smearing fat on her body. This relationship is maintained

"till she menstruated, till her breasts are developed and her pubic hair begins to show. Then he will marry her . . . The union of the two is what we might regard as the orthodox form of marriage. In other words, we have a combination of tender emotions and rape and an age difference that tends to give the male the father role" (4:104). The men direct their desire at the least threatening object they can find: a female infant. Even then, she must be raped, conquered, subdued.

7. These myths are, we must note, laden with ambivalence. They become comprehensible only when we recognize countertrends. At the end of the ritual murders, the girls and boys laugh and run off together. The purpose of the mutual intimidation was to enable each party to do that which he originally wished to do: come together. In the same way, the boys wish to join the fraternity of men to protect themselves from the devouring mother. This act only delays the inevitable. They maintain the wish to be swallowed, to enter the mother eternally. We find the original fraternal brothers encountering this destiny time and again. "Two wildcat men . . . arose in the Warramunga country. They had good stone knives and the elder brother first operated on the younger one and then the younger on the elder one They cut the ground and made a creek, and then they came to Wirrildytjirri, where they heard people crying for water. The younger brother cut the ground with his left hand and a great stream of water flowed out and with it came a big snake which first of all stood up so that its head reached into the sky; and then it ate everyone except the two wildcats . . . Again the younger brother made a creek and they kept on making creeks, and leaving spirit children, and carrying their sacred stone knives on their heads. Finally they decided to subincise themselves and to let the blood flow. After they had performed this ceremony they felt sorry and cried for their own country. The elder brother then went on to look at a waterhole which they saw in a distance, *and made a stone wurley with just a small hole at the top.* The

elder brother said, '*We want to take the blood on with us,*"
and so they went on bleeding all the way. Finally they went
into a waterhole at Baringara, and the snake coiled round
them both and took them down into the earth" (3:61).

The two brothers recapitulate much of the male defensive
cycle. They "arose" without natural parents, their only possession being knives (penis-weapon). The brothers attempt
to provide sustenance for the "people" (themselves), and to
fill up their longing for water. The gift, however, is destructive. Like the original maternal gift of the demon lore and
mythology, it carries with it a murderous, enveloping intent.
The brothers keep fending off the maternal monster. At the
same time, they try to make themselves complete by taking
on the maternal function (making spirit children). The brothers then try to become as women by altering their genitals
and letting the blood flow. The alternation of sex fails. Instead of feeling completed, they feel a sense of loss, of being
lost and of sorrow. The brothers escape the fate of being
swallowed, only to bemoan their subsequent wandering. They
then deliver themselves to the very thing they have been fleeing from: envelopment by the swallowing female monster.

8. The following description by Roheim illustrates this:
" 'Poisonous snake demon with your fangs, keep away!' A
man usually sings this when he walks to keep the snakes at
bay. In this case he was singing so that his penis should also
sing and keep the snakes from attacking it under the ground.

"The penis went into the hole and there were many rats
there. He had all the rats firmly tied, with his penis wound
right around them, and then he would tie his penis in a knot
to hold them all. Then he wound his penis round his waist
like a belt. In the evening he used to eat the rats he had se-
cured by this method. He had no spear, only his penis. But
once the penis went into a hole and there was a snake there.
The snake bit the penis, and many other snakes did the same
till the poison went right up into his heart and died.

"This identification of spearing and coitus goes very far. In

Aranda both the semen and the vaginal secretion are *inimba*. They would say with envy and respect that woman has far more inimba than man. A man has inimba only when he is actually cohabiting, a woman has it always. Then they added: 'When a man spears a woman, she becomes full of inimba' " (4:101–02).

The man manifests his fear of the devouring snake, and in defense, endows his penis with magical properties. The fear is that "my penis will be devoured in the hole": The negation is "my penis will destroy the contents of the hole." Placing one's penis in a rat's hole would not ordinarily be considered a prudent gesture. If it can become a belt or a spear, it can survive by killing the hole's owner. The ambivalent fear which calls forth the negation still remains. The man is killed by the biting snake or malevolent female symbol. Women are credited with having magical vaginal fluids, but men claim ownership of the fluid only in their transformed shape of spearer.

9. Roheim states: "There is a demon tjitji ngangarpa (baby-like), which has a head like a white smooth rock. It goes into the tnta (womb, inside stomach) and makes a person sick.

"The meaning of the penetrations of these demons into the inside, and also the fact that they develop from human emotions, is revealed by another demon, the *mangu waltalangu* (demon from a friend): a real man grows wings like an eagle hawk and flies like a demon. These demons attack women. First they eat the fat part above the vagina, then the vagina itself, and finally the whole woman. They will take any woman whether she is a close relation or not.

"Or we have the same thing in reverse. The *patiri* are demons with long teeth. They go into the baby with the mother's milk and bite the infant with their long teeth when they are inside. The demon takes the baby from the mother and eats it; the mother cries in vain. According to the Aranda belief, a man may *arelama* (bewitch by incantation) a woman so as to make her pregnant. The child that is born in consequence of this incantation is not really a child, it is a demon with long teeth. The moment it is born, it looks back at the mother. The mother dies, and the demon child disappears.

"In every man there is the child with its body destruction phantasies—the child that kills the mother with its long teeth, not by coming out of her, but by going into her" (4:57–58).

10. In ritual and behavioral counterparts of the demon lore, this voracious greed is limited by guilt and prohibition. The themes of the demon stories are enacted, or rumored to be so, by the Central Australians. Ethnographers still argue about whether these beneficient mothers kill and eat their babies. However, it is at least clear that many tribal respondents ashamedly admit to these activities, or accuse others of engaging in them. Roheim cites his field notes: "When relating one of his dreams, Pukutiwara mentioned a place called Kunnanpiri (birds' excrement). There were very many children's bones there. The children had been eaten by their mothers because they were so very thin. Then he remarked: 'Nowadays, the custom of eating children has been increasing because everything has been dry for years. The children are thin, the mothers are hungry' " (4:59).

Nor are these ideas limited to the province of dreams. Ancient tribal custom dictates that "every second child should be eaten" (4:60–61), especially if the child is born into a tribal situation where there are many children. Tribal belief indicates that devouring one child will enhance the strength of its siblings and make them grow bigger. An old woman, it was reported to Roheim, had eaten a baby sister who had been roasted by their mother. "Baby cannibalism was rife among these central-western people as it is west of the border of Central Australia. In one group east of the Murchison and Gascoyne Rivers, every woman who had a baby had killed and eaten it, dividing it with her sisters, who in turn killed their children at birth and returned the gift of food, so that the group had not preserved a single living child for some years. When the frightful hunger for baby meat overcame the mother before or at the birth of the baby, it was killed and cooked regardless of sex. But the mother never ate a child that she had allowed to live at the beginning" (4:62).

11. Roheim observes that "The parents adopt certain measures to protect the infant and the child from the demons, that is, against themselves. When the child is born, the mother-in-law cuts the daughter-in-law's hair and singes the hair of the child. If she did not do this, the hair would continue to grow and an *erintja* (demon) would eat the child (Aranda). But she also draws circles of coal around the child's face and body to protect it from the demons. The black mark makes the child ugly, and thus the demon will not eat it because it prefers to eat a 'good baby'" (4:60).

We also have indications of the process whereby parents disown their own intentions, asserting to themselves that the danger to their offspring lies "elsewhere." "Punata, a Pitjentara woman . . . had the following dreams during her pregnancy: I eat *euro* meat and then I vomit. Then I dream of a *mamu* (demon) woman who is staring at me. She has long teeth and looks like an old woman I used to know. This was *Nvingura*, a friend of my mother.

"I eat *kanjilpa* and it tastes bitter. Then I dream that a *kata kurakura* (head ugly) woman, a demon with long teeth, sits beside the windbreak and disappears. I am afraid. The demon looked like Tankai, my 'mother' (mother's sister)" (4:62–63).

12. A three- or four-year-old boy has become attached to an ethnologist's wife, and plays in her kitchen. "The *tea pot* attracted his attention. He took hold of the spout and then held his own penis. He pointed at both and said they were the same. After receiving his breakfast he promptly urinated at my wife, looking triumphant and satisfied" (4:64).

13. The fraternal heroes reinterpret their immigration as an expulsion and eternally seek vengeance on a withholding, rejecting mother. The wandering heroes thus explicitly seek

to kill the female monster. In fact, their actions always lead them to be swallowed by or merged with her. "The wandering of the two heroes is due to their mother's rejecting them, and is really based on the body destruction fantasy . . . the characteristic element is that the heroes keep taking things out of their own bodies (mucus, feces, heart, lungs, kidneys, testicles, penis, etc.) which they sometimes restore into their bodies.

"The characteristic feature of the dual unity organization is just this: the body alone represents the unity of mother and son; the separation from the body (circumcision) represents a symbolic repetition of the primal trauma, the infant torn from its mother. The myth restores, by its own means (duality of heroes), the dual unity that has been broken. But it also keeps repeating the initial trauma in the attempt to master it" (3:67).

14. This is "assured" by the initiation rites of tooth extraction and circumcision. The separated portion (tooth or foreskin) is thought to be especially durable. Thus the initiated male can ostensibly be brought back to life through reincarnation by use of this amulet. Only when so protected will the young man dare to engage in intercourse.

15. Countless variations on the initiation demonstrate the same meaning. While the initiation rite is intended to separate the boy from the maternal attachment, to let him begin anew as a son of the fraternity, "*The unconscious magic* in the ritual is, 'The child has not been severed from the mother . . .' Each novice gets a girdle with four tails hanging down. The mother sits in such a position that she can hold in her hand the tail which is attached to the left side of her son's girdle. As the novices rise to their feet at the time when they are taken away from the circle, the tails held by their mothers separated from their girdles. The mothers keep these tails and return them to their sons later on. The tail evidently symbolizes the naval cord and in a deeper sense the son's penis" (3:70).

16. According to Roheim, "(In the) . . . state of sexual tension the male projects from himself two doubles. Both are 'fathers'; that is, in order to get a girl a phantasy identification with the father has to take place.

"This is made quite certain by the fact that the boy obtains the girl by wielding a variety of the tjurunga; the namutuna and the tjurunga as such are all connected with the ancestral cult . . . in the phantasy of the love magic (the boy) identifies himself with the father" (4:110–11).

At the same time that initiation is a symbolic return to the mother, it is also merging with father. At the end of initiation, the boy no longer own his self. The penis, representing the self, has become group property. The initiates have relinquished their selves totally to their elders. This is enacted, Roheim suggests, in two ways. First the boys submit themselves to subincision (symbolic castration) by the old men of the tribe. Secondly, the removal of the foreskin is "equivalent to the son being separated from the mother" (4:88).

17. States Roheim, "The phallic element which merges into homosexuality is quite open in the songs and . . . also in the ritual . . . [T]he ritual starts with a group masturbation—not mutually, but each for himself. He must masturbate the penis until it is erect or semi-erect in order to be able to get blood from it. He jabs the subincision wound with a little piece of wood or a chip of stone and makes the blood spurt out" (4:122).

He elsewhere states, "In the ritual we have an obvious representation of the primal scene, often carried out by two males. In the central mystery of the *ngallunga* type, the fathers are telling the sons that 'we two are friends,' and in the myth the two united tjurungas figure as father and son" (4:90).

Index